# Endorsements

"There are people in all of our lives, who cross our paths—some just to cross, others to linger. Marilyn Sonmor is one who lingered and remains today in my life. She has taught many how to serve the Lord and others. Marilyn's love for the Lord is deep and it is due, I believe, because of her time in God's Word and prayer. It then is no wonder she was able to have the Lord use her to pen each chapter in this book. This is a book, worthy to be not only read, but to cause the reader to pause and reflect on one's life."

**Patti Wiens**, author of *I Praise You Because . . .* Creative Marketing Concepts, Inc. *A Child's ABC's of Praise,* Creative Marketing Concepts, Inc. and *A Child's ABC's of Thanks*

Patti Wiens is a graduate of the University of Northwestern, St. Paul, MN, with a B.S degree in Elementary Education, and a Master's degree in Educational Administration from the University of St Thomas, St. Paul, MN. She served as the administrator of New Life Academy of Woodbury MN, and received the Outstanding Educator Award from the Woodbury Chamber of Commerce. She has been a speaker and singer for numerous retreats, and her testimony, *Ordained Days* has been aired numerous times on Dr. Dobson's radio program, *Focus on the Family.*

********

"Marilyn and I were great friends while attending Northwestern College, now the University of Northwestern. Over the years we went different geographical ways. I married a missionary pilot, and my husband and I, with our three sons, were involved in three missionary adventures in unusual places over the years. Our paths crossed while our boys attended Faith Academy, the missionary boarding school in Manila and again in Phoenix, AZ for a time. *Led By An Unseen Hand* is rich in testimonies of God's leadership and God's miracles. It is a beautiful story of a beautiful family."

**Sally Pickard**, author of *Vessels of Honor & Flowers of Splendor,* Acorn Publishing. Available in hard copy and available soon on Amazon Kindle. Author of *Forgiveness from the Heart of Africa.*

Sally Pickard graduated from the University of Northwestern with a BA in Speech/Drama. She has taken courses in writing and classes in counseling at Fuller Theological Seminary. Sally and her husband, Maurice, served as missionaries with Mission Aviation Fellowship and the Liebenzell Mission in Irian Jaya, the Micronesian Islands and South Africa. She has spoken at many retreats and seminars.

# Led by an
# UNSEEN
# HAND

*A Legacy
for the Next
Generation*

## Marilyn Sonmor

WESTBOW
PRESS®
A DIVISION OF THOMAS NELSON
& ZONDERVAN

Scripture taken from the King James Version of the Bible.

Scripture taken from the New King James Version®. Copyright ©
1982 by Thomas Nelson. Used by permission. All rights reserved.

Scripture quotations marked (NIV) are taken from the Holy Bible, New
International Version®, NIV®. Copyright © 1973, 1978, 1984, 2011 by Biblica,
Inc.™ Used by permission of Zondervan. All rights reserved worldwide.
www.zondervan.com The "NIV" and "New International Version" are trademarks
registered in the United States Patent and Trademark Office by Biblica, Inc.™

Scripture quotations are taken from the Holy Bible, New Living
Translation, copyright ©1996, 2004, 2007, 2013, 2015 by Tyndale
House Foundation. Used by permission of Tyndale House Publishers,
Inc., Carol Stream, Illinois 60188. All rights reserved.

Scripture quotations are from the ESV® Bible (The Holy Bible, English
Standard Version®), copyright © 2001 by Crossway, a publishing ministry
of Good News Publishers. Used by permission. All rights reserved.

WestBow Press books may be ordered through booksellers or by contacting:

WestBow Press
A Division of Thomas Nelson & Zondervan
1663 Liberty Drive
Bloomington, IN 47403
www.westbowpress.com
1 (866) 928-1240

Because of the dynamic nature of the Internet, any web addresses or
links contained in this book may have changed since publication and
may no longer be valid. The views expressed in this work are solely those
of the author and do not necessarily reflect the views of the publisher,
and the publisher hereby disclaims any responsibility for them.

Any people depicted in stock imagery provided by Thinkstock are models,
and such images are being used for illustrative purposes only.
Certain stock imagery © Thinkstock.

ISBN: 978-1-9736-0428-0 (sc)
ISBN: 978-1-9736-0429-7 (hc)
ISBN: 978-1-9736-0427-3 (e)

Library of Congress Control Number: 2017915694

Print information available on the last page.

WestBow Press rev. date: 05/21/2019

# Contents

# Dedication

*Led By An Unseen Hand* is especially dedicated to the next generation whomever and wherever you may be. God placed a burden on my heart for you who will carry on the legacy of truth and righteous living as you face what appear to be difficult days ahead. Hopefully the evidence of God's love and care for a life lived in another time and place will give you hope no matter what the future holds. It is my desire that you will learn to trust in the One who never changes, and as a result make God your greatest friend and confidant. God desires His children to experience His best in life and He will meet all of your needs when you seek Him with your whole heart.

To *all* who follow after, along with my three children and their families, I humbly dedicate this book to you.

Tami Sonmor Engram and her husband Steve along with their sons James and Jeremey, and daughter, Kylee. (James is married to Lydia). They have a son, Peter And daughter, Leanor.

Terri Sonmor Godoy and her husband Edward along with their daughters, Jamie and Janae and son Jordan. Janae is married to Alexander Klein.

Mark Sonmor and wife Carolyn and their sons, Taylor and Chandler and daughters, Cady and Maggie. Taylor is married to Abigail. They have a daughter Olivia. Cady is married to Christian Bell.

# Foreword

*Led By An Unseen Hand* invites you to open your eyes to the work of God in your life. Sonmor gently guides you through circumstances, decisions and life changes, retelling the touch of God in the daily as well as the miraculous. Through personal stories entwined with God's precious promises in Scripture, the story reminds us that our God is present and active in every aspect of our lives.

The uniqueness in *Led By An Unseen Hand* lies in Sonmor's ability to communicate these very great and precious promises using the power of story. Recapturing events from her own life, authentically relaying the emotions of both wonder and doubt in exciting and also tragic circumstances, Sonmor provides the freedom to search for the hand of God while wrestling with Him at the same time. Throughout her life she realistically tells of her seasons where she readily embraced God's leading and direction and other times wanted to push it away, because of doubt and fear. It is her transparency within her storytelling that fills the reader with hope that God is bigger than our emotions! Our faith rests in His goodness.

Accept the invitation to journey through this memoir and be encouraged. God is leading. Even when we can't see where He is headed, His hand is upon us, directing our steps. And prayer opens our heart to the path. *Led By An Unseen Hand* provides the opportunity to walk with God more closely, allowing Him to take your hand and guide you to a future filled with wonder.

Erica Wiggenhorn, Author of *An Unexplainable Life: Recovering The Wonder & Devotion of the Early Church*, Moody Publishers

# Preface

After hearing some of my life experiences, various friends and relatives told me, "You need to write a book." This was especially true of my Aunt Louise, my mother's only sister, who kept urging me on. However, my life was always too busy it seemed, and the task was very daunting to me. I had never done anything of renown, however, God reminded me of the wonderful things *He* had done for me and I knew those things deserved to be recorded for His glory. It took many years of thought and prayer before I could begin this project. God, in fact, had to take me away from some of my other responsibilities to do this.

There is a burning desire in my heart for others to know how real God is. In one of our pastorates a woman spoke up in a women's Bible study saying, "God has never spoken to me. Has He ever spoken to any of you?" My heart was concerned that many do not experience this. God does speak, not usually in an audible voice, but a voice that we know is His. After hearing God's voice in various ways and recognizing God's hand in many areas of my life, I am deeply concerned that no one misses out on having that kind of relationship with Him. It is a very natural experience, yet one that is often neglected.

Our family of origin and the historical time period we've lived through impacts all of us. Being born in the Great Depression and growing up in poverty in a home with an alcoholic father brought some formidable circumstances to work through. Further experiences of ministry and missionary work gave many opportunities to find that God's supernatural intervention is possible in the ordinary contexts of life when we avail ourselves of the avenue of prayer. NOTHING CAN COMPARE WITH AN ANSWER TO PRAYER.

# Acknowledgments

I wish to especially acknowledge my husband Steve's special part in this project, not only for writing one of the chapters, but for his proofreading, suggestions and verifications for some parts of the book.

I also want to thank him for putting up with a less than perfect house and some skimpy meals when I was engrossed in writing. He was extremely patient through all of this and I am so thankful for him as my life partner that suffered when I suffered and rejoiced in the happy times. How wonderful it is to have a strong arm to lean on and receive a hug just when needed.

Special thanks to my son, Mark, for his expertise in answering some of my computer questions now and then as well as allowing me to use a portion of a story written during his school days, *Lost in an Uncommon Market* (in chapter 31). I am also very thankful for his willingness to take time to provide the cover design for the book. This means so much to me.

I must acknowledge my daughters, Tami Engram and Terri Godoy who have given me input on comments and suggestions. They are my "mighty mites" who work harder than anyone I know. I thank God for their wise counsel. They provided the information for chapter 44 following their recent visit to the Philippines, the land where they grew up.

Special thanks must go to David Gerbitz, my editor, who faithfully searched for errors and ways to improve the manuscript. I know God sent him to me. I also wish to acknowledge the ladies in my Prayer Intercession Team (PIT) and others from my Desert Springs Community Church family. Thanks to all who have encouraged me and prayed so faithfully. I also thank my brother, Ken Haglund, sister-in-law, Phoebe Koentopf and my cousins who provided information concerning dates and times of certain events. A huge thank you too, to Erica Wiggenhorn, a great writer and Bible Study teacher, who was willing to write the Foreword. May God bless all of you as you have blessed me.

## Special Thanks

As I considered writing my story, a dear friend, Mildred Barger, called me one day and said, "If you are planning to write that book you told me about, I will be happy to look over your manuscript and offer any help I can give." It was the nudge I needed to get going on what I was sensing God wanted me to do. Millie came into my life while I was teaching at Southwestern College, now Arizona Christian University. We worked together in the college Women's Auxiliary for several years. Millie was the secretary and helped in various ways with programs and publicity.

Millie and I also worked together on *The Women's Inspirational Network,* a paper for the Conservative Baptist women in Arizona and the surrounding Southwestern states. I attended at least one Christian Writer's Conference with Millie. She actually did something with her knowledge, having written ten books and numerous articles.

As I got to know Millie, I discovered that she had been a writer for many years. Even in grade school days her first poem was printed in a newspaper. Millie has taught in a country school and worked in various offices including a bank. She also worked as a church secretary and has been active in women's ministry. She is also known for writing and presenting dramatic readings in various settings, which she has done with excellence.

I truly believe I would not have gotten started at writing without Millie's encouragement. She has also been my prayer warrior and encourager through the entire process. God has blessed her with a sharp mind and good health even at the age of ninety-two. Millie, may God continue to give you more years to be a blessing to many as you use your talents for Him.

# Introduction

Often it isn't until after we've completed certain segments of our lives that we are fully able to understand and evaluate what we have been through. My life began during the Great Depression and though very young, I recall hearing of the bombing of Pearl Harbor as we listened to our battery-operated radio. Little did I know that many years later I was to meet the Japanese commander who led that attack and receive his autographed picture.

Our family of origin impacts us greatly. Therefore, I have included some of my family dynamics during that time in history. I am hopeful this information will provide a better understanding of the emotions and events involved in this story. Our home was riddled with poverty, alcoholism, and shame, causing me to wonder at times, "Will I survive?" It was only later in life that I really began to ask the questions, "How do I move past some of the flaws of my young life? What does God want from me? What was I created to be?

Just prior to my college graduation, I was impacted greatly when a car struck me, throwing me forty feet through the air. The injuries necessitated several weeks of hospitalization. Consequently I was not able to walk with my class at commencement. God, however, showed Himself faithful to walk with me every step of life's journey.

How my mother walked in faith victoriously through the very difficult circumstances in our home, gave me the impetus to make her faith my own, and therefore, I discovered the answers to my soul-searching questions. As I walked the steps of life's journey, God led me into the varied vocations of my life through using my gifts in music to open doors in a variety of ministry opportunities at home and abroad. My life has certainly never lacked variety as can be seen through my marriage, family, teaching experiences, pastoral ministry and Philippine missionary endeavors. Always there were unexpected experiences both joyful and problematic, which revealed to me that I had been *Led By An Unseen hand.*

# Chapter 1

## *Who Touched Me?*

Seated in the back pew on one side of my home church, First Baptist in Hastings, Minnesota, I was miserable, confused, and struggling to hold back the tears. We were in the midst of our annual missionary conference and once again the missionary speaker was pleading for volunteers to give their lives for missionary service. About a dozen missionaries had already gone out from our little church so I was well acquainted with missionary challenges. Somehow this time was different. In the past I was still young and assumed this did not apply to me. I was now out of high school and wasn't really interested but a strong conviction came to me. I wondered, *what does God want me to do? Wouldn't my sister, Hildi, be a better choice? She is more the type to be a missionary than I am. She likes learning different languages and is good at it.* However, I knew she perhaps couldn't be accepted as a missionary because of a somewhat fragile health condition in the form of a congenital heart defect.

*Could I learn another language? Could I adjust to living with people of another race and culture?* Frankly, I was somewhat repelled by the thought of it. Besides, I had so many other interests like singing and music in general. The missionary slide shows I witnessed in previous missionary presentations, showed mostly uneducated natives, and I couldn't picture them caring much about a musical message that I could offer. I got a real blessing out of ministering in music. I loved it when people expressed blessing and encouragement after I ministered in song. To me, singing was telling a story of God's love, mercy, and grace through song. It was such a joy to sing praise to God particularly for His benefit. While in high school, a course in music theory was offered one time only and at a time acceptable to my schedule. I truly enjoyed it and wanted to learn more. How could I use my music on a mission field?

I also knew missionaries had to do a lot of speaking while they are on furlough and I was extremely afraid of that. Singing brought stage fright and nervousness to the point of making me sick to my stomach. But to me, speaking was even more frightening. Besides, I didn't feel I could commit to being a missionary as a single woman. Would God really expect that of me? The more I contemplated these things, the more uncomfortable I became.

Excuses came flooding into my mind. *Lord, I am just a nobody. You know how poor and dysfunctional our family life has been.* Scenes of my childhood poured forth, days when we had nothing but lard on our homemade bread for our school lunches. All the shame of those years flooded my mind, causing me to feel sorry for myself. *Why Lord, after all I have been through here, would You send me to a place where I might have less than I did growing up? Our family didn't have electricity until I was in third or fourth grade and we never had indoor plumbing! And what about all the strange food? Lord, You know it doesn't take much of anything to upset my stomach. And Lord, is it wrong to want to live in a good house and have nice things that I never had? What kind of clothes would*

*I wear? I long to wear nice clothes, not like the hand-me-downs I've grown up with.*

At once I sensed a silent rebuke reminding me of my precious aunt Hazel who so faithfully sewed for me and she was no ordinary seamstress. She sewed for many people and did alterations for the largest department store in town. I should never complain. God had always met my clothing needs. *But how could I ever leave my family? We have all been so close as we rallied together and worked together to help one another due to my dad's alcoholism, which brought such shame to our family. I wouldn't benefit anyone if I got homesick. What if I would fail? That would be a lot of wasted money. You know I have failed You in so many ways here in America. I'm not sure I could hold out in a foreign land. I'm not that smart or well-disciplined either. I haven't been a very good witness here at home and I'm so ashamed of myself for many of the things I have done and not done. Lord, I dread trying to raise support for the mission field. Being on welfare while growing up was so embarrassing. I hate to feel needy and ask for financial support. I just feel overwhelmed by it all.*

Various verses of Scripture came to mind reminding me of God's goodness to me, how He gave all for me. I was reminded of my personal responsibility to God to follow Him at any cost. Psalm 37 had several verses that convicted me: "Delight yourself in the Lord and He shall give you the desires of your heart" (Psalm 37:4). *How could being a missionary ever give me the desires of my heart? Yet, the missionaries I listened to this week seemed as happy and joyful as anyone I've ever met.* Rereading the verse, I saw that I was *first* to delight in the Lord, *and then* He would give me the desires of my heart. There was a condition involved. I read on in Psalm 37:5: "Commit your way to the Lord, Trust also in Him and He shall bring it to pass." *Do I want this to come to pass? Does God really want me to be a missionary?* The tears continued to flow. I felt all eyes on me as if I were the only one who could accept the call.

*God, how do I know if You really want me? I don't want to go forward and volunteer if this is not for me. How do I know?* It seemed everyone was looking at me. Suddenly I felt a hand on my right shoulder. I quickly turned around to see who touched me, thinking someone must have sensed my thoughts and was going to urge me to go forward to answer the call. Turning around to look, I was simply awestruck for no one was there! I distinctly felt a hand—a gentle hand—on my shoulder. *Lord, is that You? Do you really want me?*

I really don't remember if I went forward and made an outward commitment that night to be a missionary but I knew in my heart I must continue to be attentive to the Lord's leading. Strangely, I never told anyone about the touch on my shoulder. I guess, in a way, it was something too sacred, something between God and me. And I think a part of me did not want to let anyone know because I doubted they would believe me. Then too, if anyone knew of it, I would somehow be more accountable to follow through. I did remember telling the Lord I would plan to move forward toward the mission field unless He showed me differently.

Actually, it was only in recent years that I even mentioned this special touch to my husband and family. Years later this experience came back to me as I read these words: "You have laid your hand upon me. Such knowledge is too wonderful for me, too lofty for me to attain. Where can I go from your Spirit? If I go to the heavens, you are there, if I make my bed in the depths, you are there. If I rise on wings of the dawn, if I settle on the far side of the sea, even there your hand will hold me fast" (Psalm 139:5b-10). Truly, the knowledge was too wonderful and lofty for me to attain, and yes, there were times I wanted to escape from God's presence and not face the issue of obedience.

I continued to search the Word of God, and once again He spoke to me saying, "Rest in the Lord, and wait patiently for Him" (Psalm 37:7a). I knew that was all I could do as I didn't yet have finances to enter college full time. I was still working in an office in my hometown trying to build my college fund. It was then that verse 23 of Psalm 37 spoke to me: "The steps of a good man are ordered by the Lord. And He delights in his way." I knew I had to patiently wait and take each step with Him.

I checked a few colleges to make sure where God wanted me. I applied to Moody Bible Institute as there was no tuition cost there. However, they were full at that time and not taking new students for the coming year. I also considered Bethel College in St. Paul, Minnesota where Hildi attended, but God gave no peace in my heart regarding that. So it was with patience and determination that I set about saving for the day when I could enter Northwestern College where I believed God was directing me. "The hand of our God is for good to all who seek Him" Ezra 8:22b).

# Chapter 2

*Family Matters*

Though eager to get on with God's call on my life, I valued those days that I could spend with my family while I continued to work toward my goals. Family does matter and I believe God works through the family setting to shape and mold our lives into what His creative purpose is for His children.

God gave me a wonderful family to love, but we were not without our difficulties. My father, John Haglund, of Swedish descent, grew up in a very strict home and as a result had many good things to teach us regarding manners, respect, hard work and responsibility. A good musician, he was my chief encourager when it came to my interest in music. He had the gift of playing any instrument by ear and had a great singing voice. His primary instrument was the guitar and he even taught some lessons. In their early years, he and my mom played in a church string band along with his sisters and one of mom's brothers. Dad played the guitar, and Mom played the mandolin.

Mom, Mary Magdalene by name, was always called "Helen" due to a schoolteacher's mistake. At home she was called Lena pronounced "Lay-nah" taken from the last syllable of Magdalene. Apparently because her mother's name was Maria, they chose to use her middle name. The teacher thought "Lay-nah" was short for "Helena" resulting in the teacher calling her "Helen." Apparently it stuck for the rest of her life. It always seemed strange that my parents' common names, John and Mary were so confusing. Dad's middle name was Reuben and since he was John, Jr. his family decided to call him Reuben. My mom's family called him "Jack" to differentiate him from mom's oldest brother who was also named John. Though they meant to make things clearer, it didn't work out that way.

My parents, John and "Helen" Haglund

Mom's grandparents came from Germany while Dad's parents came from Sweden; consequently traditions from both countries were carried out in our home, particularly at Christmas time.

Dad, a carpenter by trade, built quite a few homes in our town but sadly we as a family didn't see much of what he earned. His music abilities lured him into a worldly scene of entertainment that eventually led him into alcoholism. This was the underlying cause of our difficulties emotionally, economically and spiritually.

Mom came to know Christ through Dad's family which was very godly, albeit very strict. My grandfather, after building a new barn, invited an evangelist from Minneapolis to hold an evangelistic meeting in the barn prior to storing hay for the winter. It was there that my mother and her mother, Grandma Feldhahn, gave their lives to Christ. My dad, however, rebelled against the strictness of his parents and went into a world of supposed pleasure and its many sinful vices. This eventually created a rift between Mom and Dad. Their philosophies of life became totally opposite. While Dad was enjoying the worldly pleasures, Mom's sad lot in life and her needy heart drew her closer to God causing her to become a very godly woman of prayer. It was God who became her source of strength.

Though very quiet, Mom was a hard-working woman. Things would sometimes get especially quiet in the house. It was then that we would find Mom in her bedroom on her knees in prayer. I couldn't have asked for a more loving, self-sacrificing mom. Some of her favorite sayings were, "Life is too short to quarrel," "Where there is a will there is a way," "Haste makes waste," and "A watched pot never boils." She was not a stylish woman but a truly meek, unselfish person who spoke no evil of anyone. As one neighbor testified, "I never heard her speak a derogatory word about anyone." Many are the lessons she taught us by her sweet disposition and faithfulness.

Mom loved to bake and her homemade bread was a favorite for everyone who was privileged to sample it. I especially loved her hot biscuits with just plain butter. When I came home from college on the bus, she usually timed the baking so she was taking them out of the oven when I walked in the door. My college roommates who occasionally came home with me often remarked about her wonderful bread and brownies.

We would have been quite a family if all Mom's babies had lived. Their first baby was born without a spine and lived only a short time.

The next child, Hildegard, (Hildi, as we called her), was born with a hole in her heart that kept her from engaging in any strenuous activities. After many physical tests in various hospitals, my parents were told there was no surgery or anything that could correct her problem. Hildi was the tallest in our family and had the lightest hair color of all of us siblings. However, she had a sort of blue complexion due to her heart problem and this of course caused her much grief. She was unable to engage in sports and do many of the things others could do. Instead, she poured her efforts into her studies and earned very good grades. She was especially proficient in secretarial skills that helped her readily find good employment. She loved to sing and we often sang duets.

The Feldhahn Homestead

I guess Hildi didn't like my music!

Both Hildi and I were born in Wilson, Wisconsin, in the same old farmhouse in which my mother was born. It was the Feldhahn family's homestead that had been in the family for a number of decades. I was born in the month of January and according to Aunt Louise Rasmussen, Mom's sister, I arrived before a doctor could get there. Aunt Louise said she was the one who cut the umbilical cord. It was at the height of the Great Depression and phones were rare in most rural homes at that time. I am not sure a doctor ever arrived but God was gracious and to my knowledge, I was my parents' first healthy baby. When I was about two years old, our family moved from Wisconsin to Hastings, Minnesota. In spite of Hildi's health, we were constant companions. She didn't enjoy playing house with dolls as I did, but she would play paper dolls with me. I particularly enjoyed making my paper dolls into twins by creating a matching outfit for one of them. Having grown up at the time of the Dionne Quintuplets, (five identical sisters) who, by the way, were often pictured in paper doll kits, I was very intrigued with look-alike people.

By the time we had lived in four different places in Hastings, two baby boys were born prematurely and lived only briefly. Three years after my birth, another boy, Kenneth Roger, was born. He was a healthy, chubby little boy with lots of golden curls that later turned dark brown. We moved to an apartment above a store on Main Street when Ken was about three years old. I was in kindergarten at the time and recall walking home from school one day and falling into an uncovered manhole. Fortunately, I was wearing a snowsuit so didn't get too cold. As I tried to climb out, a black man appeared to help me. I had never seen him before and we only knew of one black man in our town at that time and this wasn't him.

Ken, when about two or three years old, wandered out of the apartment in the middle of the night and was found down by the railroad station. All of us were sleeping soundly with our doors open due to the summer heat. Mom was shocked to answer a knock at the door and find a black man holding Ken and asking, "Is this your boy?" Mom said she nearly fainted. Again, we didn't know this black man or how he knew where to bring my wandering little brother, but have wondered to this day if he was a guardian angel to Ken and me.

Living downtown gave us some interesting experiences like watching circus parades march through town, staring at the gypsies that gathered on one of the corners on main street and watching the steamboats come down the Mississippi river under our world-famous spiral bridge with the familiar sounds of their steam whistles and calliopes. I will always remember an excursion down the Mississippi to Red Wing, Minnesota, which our dear aunts, Esther and Hazel Haglund, supplied for us.

Aunt Esther and Hazel

When I was five and Hildi seven, our aunts also took Hildi and me shopping in St. Paul, Minnesota, where we got the first edition of *Rudolph the Red-Nosed Reindeer* put out by Montgomery Ward and Company. It was the first time Hildi and I had seen black women. To me they looked extremely tall. I wondered, *are they real people? Yes, they must be they could move their eyes and speak.* This may sound strange to folks of our day but at age five years old, in my limited area of the world, this was actually what went through my mind. Today I hardly notice the difference in skin color and have many good friends among them all.

Hildi and I went to Sunday School from preschool on. We so enjoyed our little pink Sunday School papers we received each Sunday along with a little card with a

Scripture verse depicting some of Jesus' many activities while here on earth. I thank God for those early memories of Jesus and learning to pray at a tender age. Surely the Lord ordered those steps.

# Chapter 3

$\mathcal{N}$

## *Little House on the Prairie*

While we lived at the downtown apartment, Dad was building our first home. We have since called this home our "little house on the prairie" as it was located on Sixth and Prairie Streets. West of us we could see only farmland, yet in the other directions many new homes were going up. When we first moved in, there were dingy wood laths on the walls waiting to be plastered, no electricity and no ceilings so we could see into the rafters and the attic above us. We would often climb into the attic and jump onto our beds below—when no one was looking of course! My childhood friend, Jan Niederkorn, recently wrote me a note reminding me of the fun sleepovers we had together at her house or mine.

The little house in the early days

The house several years later

Jan lived on third and Prairie Street so we were close. I would often go to piano lessons with Jan or my other friend, Beverly Van Campen, who lived on Sixth Street. How I longed to play the piano and would attempt to do so whenever I was in their homes. Bev's mom played the piano and loved to sing. I loved to hear her sing the alto part in their church choir. She was a beautiful woman and very kind to us. I always regard her as one of my early role models. It wasn't long until I was learning to harmonize. When Bev and I were in the sixth grade, we sang a duet for our class where I added the harmony on "If you should Go to Venice," a simple rendition of *A Viennese Melody.*

Ken was fascinated with every part of our house coming together in stages. Dad gave him a hammer and a bunch of nails and let him pound as many nails as he wanted into the chimney wall knowing it would one day be totally covered. Dad loved his only son and soon Ken was also learning to strum Dad's guitar while Dad did the fingering. Dad would take him into a tavern and they'd sing, "This Little Boy of Mine, He loves me all the time. He sits upon my knee and plays guitar with me." Ken would proudly come home with a pocket full of change. Hildi and I felt Ken was getting spoiled. We remember the day he got a tricycle and a red wagon all on the same day when we got nothing. I'm sure we were to share it but that really wasn't appropriate for us. Hildi, so upset with the whole thing, socked Ken and gave him a nosebleed. Not knowing how to explain it to Dad, she blamed it on the neighbor kids and I guess neither my folks nor Ken ever knew what hit him!

When I was about six years old, we had an unforgettable experience of having a "Quarantined" sign placed on our front door, as the doctor believed I had scarlet fever. I recall being placed in a baby crib in the living room so I'd be near the stove. In the end, they said it was a false alarm and it was only a bad case of tonsillitis. It was recommended that I have a tonsillectomy, which never happened since my family could not afford it. Close to that time, I also got chicken pox and whooping cough along with the rest of my siblings.

The memories of this little house included attending a one-room schoolhouse for grades one to three. It was one of three such schools strategically placed so that young children wouldn't have to endure the otherwise long walk to the public school. As it was, Hildi still had to get a ride with a neighbor in the winter months, as the walk was too much for her. One teacher taught all three grades. Our particular teacher had been there so long, she had taught many of the parents. Those days brought memories of old fashioned desks with inkwells. My next teacher's name was Miss Palmer, one of my favorites. I thought for a while that she had invented the Palmer method of cursive writing. We were never taught to print as it just came naturally. At the back of the room was a large wood furnace. Near the front entrance was a cloakroom, which also contained a huge water jug that was delivered by the janitor each morning. Toilets were in a large coal shed behind the school.

Recess play was very memorable as we played with jacks, marbles, jump rope and various forms of tag. There was also a slide and swings on the playground. One day while enjoying recess, we saw an old car running all over the playground without a driver. We all ran for the front steps of the school. Eventually the car ran into a tree where it sputtered to a stop. My dad's cousin, Ted Olson, who lived nearby, came and shut the motor off. We found that the man living next to the school had cranked his car to get it started and didn't realize it was in gear. The car ran over him but somehow he escaped any injuries.

On another occasion, we heard the clouds were going to burst. We were scared to death and ran to a home nearby and knocked at the door. Some student, braver than I, explained that we were there because the clouds were going to burst. The lady of the house assured us that just means it is going to rain and we'd better high-tail it back to school! The teacher wondered why no one responded to the bell she so forcefully rang.

Memories of the little house included gathering in our living room at night around the kerosene lamplight, listening to our battery-operated radio. Dad loved to listen to "Amos and Andy," "Lum and Abner," and the "Sunset Valley Barn Dance." We kids loved "Henry Aldrich" and a few others. Another nice memory was having Dad get out his guitar and play and sing for us. He played hymns as well as popular tunes of the day.

Perhaps the most vivid memory was hearing about the bombing of Pearl Harbor and all of the news related to World War II. We had the rationing of butter, sugar, coffee and other products like rubber. Instead of elastic where it ought to be in our underclothing we had buttons or ties. We were young enough to remember but not really old enough to understand the full significance of that difficult time in history. It was also the time of green and gold bond stamps given as premiums for certain purchases that could be redeemed for merchandise at various locations.

Our sister Gladys was born while living in this little house on the prairie. Glady, as we affectionately called her, was a happy, sanguine child who grew up learning to sing and tell fun little stories. She brought so much life and fun to our home as a bright-eyed happy child. As we grew older, she and I were mistaken for each other though I was almost eight years older. However, I was always considered the serious one by my father while she was the fun-loving, carefree one.

Mom, Glady, Hildi, Marilyn & Ken

With our Wisconsin cousins and friend, Bev

One of the blessings we had as children, was having our cousins visit us from the country. Aunt Louise and Uncle Marvin Rasmussen lived on a farm south of Hammond, Wisconsin, in an area called Pleasant Valley. To us, it was just that—a pleasant, happy, get-away. We loved to spend a week or two on the farm with our cousins: Mavis, three months older than me, Vernon, one year younger than me, followed by Colleen, Ken's age, Arlice, younger still and Jim, a year and a half younger than Arlice. He was Glady's age. We usually got together for a big Fourth of July picnic and as darkness set in Dad would set off the fireworks he brought along for the evening. These were as big as any we used to see at the county fairs and what fun we had until someone stepped with bare feet on a sparkler carelessly thrown to the ground.

Airplanes were beginning to show up more and more at that time and I remember Vern running outside at the sound of every airplane. They weren't seen as often out in the country where they lived. He eventually became a pilot in the air force and later a commercial pilot. Even yet, in his retirement years, airplanes continue to occupy his mind.

The time on the farm taught us much about hard work as well as carefree fun: climbing in the hay mow, playing hide and seek, bringing the cows home, swimming in the creek and attending 4H meetings with our cousins. How can I ever forget Colleen falling from high in the hay mow down to the main floor of the barn and Uncle Marvin leaping over the barnyard fence when he heard Vern say, "Colleen's dead." Amazingly, she wasn't hurt. Apparently some hay accompanied her for a somewhat soft landing.

We attended Vacation Bible School at their little country church where classes were held in the country school across the street. I recall doing a lot of Scripture memorization. We also had a time of recess where we often ended up playing near the cemetery behind the church. In the evening hours we played outside and enjoyed catching lightning bugs once darkness set in. Best of all they had a piano and Aunt Louise knew how to play it.

Our cousins equally enjoyed their time in the city with us. Our town had several factories, a flourmill, a dam on the river and a lot of things that were new to them. They also attended our Vacation Bible School and enjoyed getting to know some of our friends. I don't know how we all fit in our small bedrooms and beds but we managed and never complained.

A few sad memories came to my counsins' family when Uncle Marvin got sick with Hodgkin's disease and passed away at thirty-nine years of age. Very shortly after his death, Arlice passed away from a ruptured appendix. This was one of our first experiences with death. We felt so sad for our dear, sweet, Aunt Louise and all the cousins. God gave them strength, however, as He always does in times of deep distress. They moved to another farm for a while and then to River Falls, Wisconsin where they all finished high school, furthered their education, and moved on to their careers and eventually marriage. We have always been close.

Aunt Louise was the youngest in Mom's family and her only sister, but she had several brothers. Uncle John, her oldest brother often did carpenter jobs with Dad and would stay with us occasionally. He also sold Watkins products, so was quite well known in his area. The others were Otto, William, Herman, Frank, and Joe. Uncle Frank was the only brother who married.

Uncle Frank and Aunt Annie's farm was very near our birthplace and we also enjoyed their children, Patricia, Francis and Larry. They later moved to St. Paul, Minnesota where we continued to see them occasionally. The attraction at their house was an antique piano with a totally flat top that looked more like a table. Uncle Frank played the violin and was in the string band with my mom and dad. Larry, their youngest was a victim of bulbar polio that was so prevalent in our youth. Mom made sure we prayed for him daily for several years while he, as a young boy, was in an iron lung. Larry grew up and did well but in later years has suffered with post-polio problems. That family is also very special to us.

Uncle Joe, the youngest brother, played the flute. Both Otto and Willy were in the First World War as was my father. Dad was discharged shortly, however, because he got the horrible flu that killed so many soldiers at that time.

One summer while we visited on our cousin's farm, Mom, Dad, and Glady came to bring us back home and we found to our surprise our house was finished inside and out. What a contrast to see white plastered walls with archways and beautiful tile in the kitchen. Dad had done a beautiful job. We truly felt like we were in a palace compared to the dingy brown lathes that had previously covered the walls. Electricity was put in and a basement was dug. We never did have running water other than a cistern, but it was at least helpful for doing the laundry. There was still no refrigerator—just an icebox for which we had a solid block of ice delivered periodically.

Dad took great pride in our yard, which was adorned with climbing roses, tulips, irises and other lovely flowers. We loved our weeping willow tree, apple trees and our huge garden. The soil was especially good and people would drive by admiring our lovely produce in the garden. We admired it too but didn't always enjoy the hoeing, weeding, picking off potato bugs, picking strawberries and peddling them around the neighborhood. Mom had lots of canning to do every summer and fall. We had to help as much as possible and how thankful we were to have food stored in the basement for the winter months, for often that is all we had.

While living at this house we continued attending Sunday school and church even though we kids had to ride in the back of our neighbor's truck. As we got a little older we were able to walk the mile and a half distance.

It was on a Sunday evening when I went to church by myself that I made the most important decision of my life. I began to realize as the pastor spoke, he was describing my life without Christ. I had been in Sunday school for years but never realized until the age of eight, that I needed to accept Jesus personally as my Savior. I knew He died for me but never realized that I needed to respond by accepting that payment for my sin. In later years I came to understand more of what it meant to live for Christ. I was the first to go forward that night when the invitation was given to those who wanted to accept Jesus as personal Savior. My friend Jan and a few others followed and arrangements were made for us to be baptized soon. I came home and immediately told Mom about it. Hildi was very intrigued and asked many questions so Mom led her to Christ at home. She was baptized along with me as well as Jan and others of my friends.

When I was baptized, the pastor asked me if I had a Scripture verse I would like to share. I wasn't prepared for that so I simply said my memory verse for Sunday School that day which was Acts 26:19: "Therefore, King Agrippa, I was not disobedient to the heavenly vision." I noticed everyone was snickering and I was embarrassed wondering if this was the wrong kind of verse to share. It wasn't till years later that I fully realized the occasion for that verse in Scripture and what it meant. I guess the snickering was partly because at eight years old, I was too small to be seen over the baptistery. Though I was young, I have never doubted my salvation. I have failed the Lord many times and at an older age, I needed to renew my commitment to follow Jesus more fully.

# Chapter 4

## *Tough Times*

It was difficult to move away from our "little house on the prairie." We had to sell the house due to economic problems largely due to Dad's alcoholism and the depression, which made it difficult to find work.

The big, old house

The actual move took place when I was away helping one of our relatives. I came home excitedly announcing that I had earned fifty cents. However, my words echoed through the empty house. I knew where we were moving but didn't know it would be that day. Taking a look at my beloved little house and neighborhood, I set out walking sadly to my next home. It was an old house across from a large city park where there was playground equipment, a tennis court, and further down the street, was the football field and stadium. It was a great place for picnics and we had several family reunions there. The house itself left much to be desired as it had no insulation and was very cold in the winter. God was faithful in spite of circumstances and brought new friends to the area. How we thanked the Lord for lasting friends and the stability of our church family.

I was now in sixth grade, Hildi in eighth, Ken in third, while Glady was about to begin kindergarten. I remember so well taking Glady to register for school on her golden birthday, being four on the fourth of September in 1944. I was so proud to introduce her to the same teacher I had in kindergarten. When Miss Casserly asked Glady when her birthday was, she shyly answered, "Today."

Glady gave us many laughs and consequently brought cheer to our home. One day while Aunt Hazel was working at the telephone office switchboard in town and saw someone calling from our number, she asked the usual question: "Number please?" When Glady gave the number of the police, Aunt Hazel asked, "Glady, why are you calling the police? She said, "Ken won't play house with me." Aunt Hazel, knowing the policeman who lived up the street from us rang his number and briefed him a bit as to what was going on. The policeman decided to play along with it and came asking for Ken and scared him half to death. I guess he thought he'd better attempt to obey whether he liked it or not. This is just one of the mischievous things this little sister did. But oh, how we all loved her.

Glady grew up loving to write and draw cartoons.

She played clarinet in the band and became the junior band's shortest member. Band became her main interest throughout her school days. She loved her clarinet, which she dubbed "Clarabelle Swabcase." At one of her marching band events, she had the privilege of shaking hands with President Eisenhower. She didn't get into singing as much as Hildi and I until her college years. It was then that Hildi, Ken, Glady and I formed a quartet and occasionally sang in churches and youth meetings.

Some of the most common things of the day gave us entertainment and enjoyment. At noon, we listened to "Cedric Adams and The Noon-Time News" and the daily mystery of "Old Ma Perkins." That was a time when Dad would enter in with us seeking to solve all Ma Perkin's mysteries. Other radio programs were "The Butternut Coffee House Party" and Art Linkletter's program with kids. Simple things shaped our days since there was no TV at that time. I remember when one of our neighbors got one of the first black and white TV's but the picture was nothing but a blur. It was not nearly as thrilling as listening to the radio and filling the stories with our imagination.

By this time we had a party-line phone and had acquired a refrigerator. Later we got a bottle gas range but for a long time we had only a kerosene stove which on one occasion almost caught the house on fire. Mom had to pick it up and throw it out into a snow bank singeing her hair a bit in the process.

Time progressed and long after we thought we were through with babies at our house, we noticed mom was pregnant again. At this time Dad had gone to the Twin Cities to find work so he was not home much at all. Ken, as young as he was, had to help mom haul oil home from the gas station in his wagon to keep our home heated.

We noticed Mom getting up during the night with

difficulty breathing. Hildi had to take the lead and call our aunts who in turn got mom into the hospital. While she was there we stayed with our aunts, Esther and Hazel. Mom had a bad case of albumen of the kidneys and could have died. She gave birth prematurely to another little girl, Carol Louise, who lived for only two or three days. We never got to see her but Aunt Hazel said she was beautiful.

Soon after Mom got home from the hospital, she didn't seem right and Hildi called a pastor for help. Mom had gone into post-partum depression and had to be put into a mental hospital for several months while we again went to stay with our aunts. This was a trial for all concerned and put a lot of economic pressure on our aunts. We kids all felt the shame and sadness of this difficult time, but praise God, He is always faithful and once again met our needs. He brought Mom back home to us and from then on, she shared more openly with us rather than keeping her trials to herself. She needed us to understand what she was going through and we all learned to pray diligently for each other, particularly for our dad. In our early teens, we became grounded more thoroughly in our faith and knew we had to depend on God for all things.

I used to ask the Lord, *Why does our family have to suffer so much?* One of my most embarrassing moments was when, in front of the whole class, a fellow student asked if that was my dad's truck that was always parked in front of a certain bar in town. I was so ashamed; I said it wasn't even though Dad's name was written in big, bold letters on the side of the truck. I knew it was a lie and that was one thing we knew we'd be punished most harshly for but I simply couldn't face my classmates. Dad's sisters were also deeply hurt by their brother being known as one of the town's drinking bums.

Sometimes we didn't have enough food and our aunts would bring us something to eat. We would never have had Christmas if it weren't for those two dear aunties bringing us gifts piled on a sled singing, "Jingle Bells" and shouting "Ho Ho Ho" pretending to be Santa as they came. Neither of them ever learned to drive a car.

Dad would often go off to a tavern on Christmas Eve refusing to go with us to be with his cousins and sisters. After the night was over, he ranted and raved at all of us for not including him in our Christmas celebration. Though it hurts me to say it, I don't remember ever getting a Christmas gift from him.

Finally we went on welfare, which my mom detested. She wanted her husband to love her and provide for the family. At one point she had to testify before the courts and he was put in jail for not supporting the family. Many people told Mom she should leave him but she would always answer, "No, I vowed before God that I would remain with him no matter what the conditions were." *Why, oh why,* I would ask, *is all of this happening in our high school years when it makes it so difficult to have friends over?* What friends we did have were afraid of him and really didn't want to come to our house and others we were too ashamed to invite.

Ken, now fifteen, began yearning to drive a car. He decided he would motorize his bicycle in spite of Dad forbidding him to do so. He took it for a spin one day riding though the cemetery on the quiet trails located there. As he drove out the gate he was hit by a pickup truck and was severely injured. One leg was broken in several places. He had at least eight weeks in the hospital with his leg in traction. When it was over, he tried to stand and crumpled to the floor in weakness. To this day he knows he should have obeyed our dad. Often, due to our lack of respect for Dad, we didn't think it was necessary to obey him. We all had lessons to learn.

One day as I mulled over our problems, a new thought entered my mind and I was able to thank God for all the troubles and trials. I looked around at many of my classmates who seemed to have everything going for them, yet many were making wrong choices and their lives were heading in a downward path. But for the grace of God, I knew I would choose wrongly too. As it was, I had many sins I had to confess to the Lord and only He knows the heartache I bear because of them. I recognized, however, these troubles and trials had forced me to turn to the Lord and trust Him for the future.

While in high school I was constantly out to prove myself, to show others I could do something worthwhile. I worked hard to become a First Class Girl Scout, participated in plays, choir, operettas, cheerleading, became the drum majorette for the band, and was a member of several organizations. I wanted to do everything possible to be "like everyone else" or at·least not looked down upon. There was always the fear of not measuring up or fitting in. Dad always showed his pride in me when I did things that showed and would take pictures of me leading the band for special parades in our town. I suppose it is common for all youth to desire to be noticed and be successful. I know I was allowing my own desires to consume me rather than putting sufficient time on my schoolwork. I'm sure I could have done much better if I had disciplined myself. God had to show me how He saw me. My life was mostly full of pretense and misplaced values.

Then God put in my heart the desire for the things that really count in life. It took time, but God had to bring emptiness out of the things I thought were my greatest joys. When I was offered a chance to attend a Christian high school in my senior year, my mom was willing to help with the tuition though it was a great sacrifice. I attended Minnehaha Academy where I took more music theory, sang with the Minnehaha Singers, and enjoyed the Christian atmosphere.

God provided opportunities to serve in the Twin City and state youth work, teaching me leadership and dependence on Him by serving as an officer. I learned much about organizing events and taking responsibility. It also provided new friendships and broadened my knowledge while chipping away on my insecurities and pride and molding me for what was ahead.

While living at home, Mom taught me how to read notes in a score of music and Dad taught me how to play chords. My friend Jan's parents gave us their old upright piano but some of the keys were stuck. Dad took it all apart, glued some of the hammers and hung them on a makeshift clothesline in the living room. Later he put it all back together and tuned it according to his own ear! We learned a lot on that old piano. Later Hildi and I purchased a good, second-hand piano, which was a dream come true for all of us. Having inherited Aunt Hazel's violin, I also took some violin and piano lessons from a very godly woman in our church. I felt this would further prepare me for my studies in music. It was a blessing being in this dear woman's presence. I remember walking home from her house at night, usually on snowy nights, praying aloud while gazing at the sky, thanking God for all that He had done for me. I sought to get all of the dross out of my life and God knew I had plenty to deal with. Many times I would reach home and not want to go in as I was having such a precious time with the Lord. That was a time when I sensed I was having a personal revival and cleansing in my soul. God was preparing me in so many ways.

I was still sewing most of my clothes and really needed a new sewing machine. Our old treadle machine was not doing a good job. I noticed in our hometown paper, a contest to win a sewing machine, which involved counting the dots in a certain picture. I knew I had to win that machine somehow. I drew lines throughout the picture and counted the dots in each section and added them together. Lo and behold, I won the contest and I also got a coupon to buy a second machine at half-price. Knowing Aunt Hazel also needed a new machine, I gave her the coupon and she was blessed with a new machine as well.

During this time of waiting, I also began taking voice at Northwestern College from Oliver Mogck, a great singer and vocal coach as well as a marvelous man of God. I had a half-day off from work each week so I would take the train to Minneapolis each Friday for my lesson. Often I would also have to take the train to various meetings in Minneapolis where I would have to spend the night. I would usually stay with my Minnehaha classmate, Joyce Hedwall (now Trebilco) who later became a missionary to Vietnam and Indonesia. I got off at the Washington Avenue train station, located in the skid row area of the city. One particular night there were several men standing on the corner and a black man approached me desiring to know where I was going to get off so he could watch over me. He said he didn't trust all of these men that were going to be on that bus. Afterwards I wondered why I trusted *him* but something told me he was a kind man and really did have my best interest at heart. Could this be my black guardian angel again? I did arrive safely.

I could hardly wait to be in college, however, there was one more thing I knew I needed to do at home and that was to purchase new living room furniture for my family.

31

I knew it would dip into my college fund, but I happened to find a really good deal on a room of furniture, which of course was nothing fancy, but at least would make our home more presentable. We still had to put up with stovepipes in the living room but at least the stove was removed during the summer months, which was always a pleasant relief. My parents lived with that furniture the rest of their lives.

Glady, Ken, Marilyn and Hildi

# Chapter 5

*The Test*

The day finally came when my college fund seemed adequate to get started for one semester. It was the middle of the year and though I would rather have begun in the fall, I felt I could perhaps have enough for one semester and then work in the summer to prepare for the next year's tuition. It was January 1954, I had just turned twenty-one, and was finally ready to begin my college adventure.

Registration came a bit earlier than opening day of classes and I began to wonder what I should choose as my major. I was reminded of that touch on my shoulder at the missions conference and I didn't feel I could discount missions, yet I was torn between that and music. I remember praying, *Lord, please speak to me through Mr. Mogck at my next voice lesson and tell me what I should do about declaring a major.*

As my next lesson was in progress I wondered how I should approach Mr. Mogck with my question, when suddenly he asked my accompanist to leave early because he wanted to talk to me. My heart began to beat a bit faster as I realized this might be God's answer. I thought I would have to ask *him* but instead he was asking *me* what I felt God wanted me to do with my life. I proceeded to tell him my concern for missions and yet the thought of studying music was still tugging at my heart. I explained my dilemma about registration and choosing a major. He said God had given me a gift and when God gives us a gift, He wants us to develop it and use it to the fullest for His glory.

Mr. Mogck then gave me an assignment: He said, "I want you to go by Schmidt Music Store today and pick up a current copy of *The Etude* – a classical music periodical. There's an article there entitled 'Careers of Service in Sacred Song' written by George Beverly Shea. I believe after you read this article you will know what God wants you to do." He also explained that by studying music, I was not closing the door to missions. He explained how music could be used anywhere in the world for God's glory. I still wondered exactly how it could be used in such primitive and remote places, but I assumed he knew more about that than I did.

As I left the music studio that day, I felt I was walking on the proverbial cloud nine. I had not yet gotten to read the article but I had a definite answer to prayer. God answered exactly at the time and place and through the person I requested. The more I thought about it, the more wonderful it became. God cared enough about me to answer that specific prayer, which gave me courage and the knowledge of how much God loved me and cared for the very details of my life.

On the train ride home that day, I delved into the article by Bev Shea and knew that God was leading me in the next step of my life, to set out to major in music, which was the love of my life. Psalm 37:23 came to mind again reminding me, "The steps of a good man are ordered by the LORD, and He delights in his way." Yes, this was a step—only the first step—but I knew it was a step in the right direction.

God was so marvelous to give me the joy of an answered

prayer so specifically in my young life. Doubtless He knew this experience would give me courage in years to come. I believe God desires for all of His children to know how real and personal He is so we will trust Him fully. How often God reminds me of this answered prayer to make me aware of His great love, grace, and guidance.

I recalled an Old Testament story found in Judges 6:11-20, that a man of God named Gideon had prayed a similar type prayer asking for specific conditions at a specific time. Gideon, in order to determine God's leading, asked God to first cause the fleece of wool on the threshing floor to have dew on it and the ground around it to be dry. Then Gideon would know that God would use him to save Israel. It happened as Gideon had asked. But Gideon still wanting greater assurance, requested God, apologetically this time, to have the fleece be dry and the ground to be wet with dew. God was gracious and answered just as Gideon had requested. I've heard some folks criticize Gideon, saying he had a lack of faith. Upon examining this passage, I believe praying intentionally as Gideon did, required great faith. Gideon had a background of Baal worship and didn't have a great deal of experience with the living God. At any rate, God knew Gideon's heart and honored his request. God knows each of us intimately. As He did for Gideon, He did for me and it encouraged me in my faith for years to come.

# Chapter 6

## College Days

Attending Northwestern College was like a dream come true. Many of the professors and students had often participated in the services of my home church. I had yearned to be a part of that wonderful place where Billy Graham had recently served as president. I thought of Northwestern as a next-to-heaven place where everyone truly loved the Lord and exemplified Christ. I was warned, however, that all students in Bible Colleges are not necessarily spiritually mature and some may even be there against their will. I was warned to choose my friends wisely.

I was blessed with wonderful roommates and many new friends as the college provided many opportunities for an interesting social life. It's no wonder it was often referred to as Northwestern "Bridal" College. This had its advantages and disadvantages as it often interfered with our study hours. I found that after being out of school for two and one-half years I needed to learn to discipline myself and that took some time to figure out. I also found that most of the guys in my classes were younger than I and when it came to dates, they all seemed a bit immature. Nevertheless, I had many good times and learned a lot.

Because Northwestern had a radio station, we were

some of the first to hear about the five missionary martyrs who were slain in the jungles of Ecuador. I will never forget hearing the news as we roamed the halls in a daze. One of those martyrs, Roger Youderian, was a graduate of Northwestern, so this hit very close to the hearts of all of us. Naturally, there was a plea for more missionaries to replace those who had perished. This event had a sobering effect on the entire student body.

Besides school, I of course had to find a job to pay for my continuing college expenses. I had several short-term jobs, one in a mission office, and eventually as a part-time secretary at Fourth Baptist Church where Dr. R.V. Clearwaters was pastor as well as a member of the College Board. I worked there most of my freshman and sophomore years. Many Northwesterners attended that church and I became very active in the youth ministry as well as in the music. Dr. Bill Berntsen, chairman of the Music Department at Northwestern was the music director at the church as well. God used that time to teach me the inner workings of the church as I did the church bulletin, typed the youth paper, ran the mimeograph machine, handled many phone calls, and took dictation for letters and typed a good share of a book Dr. Clearwaters wrote. However, the job was not going to last forever as I had been replacing the full-time secretary who had been ill. She eventually recovered enough so that she could be back full time. Once again I looked for employment and found work in a life insurance office. I worked in three different life insurance offices before graduation.

A few hours in the evening I tended the college switchboard. The woman who worked it full-time lived near the college in a home with other women. On several occasions she requested me, through our Christian work department, to give a devotional talk to the ladies. This was a new adventure for me though I had given devotional messages to my church youth group before. On the first occasion, God led me to speak on Psalm 28:7, "The Lord is my strength and my shield; My heart trusted in Him, and I am helped; Therefore my heart greatly rejoices; And with my song will I praise Him." I showed how that verse had come to mean much to me by emphasizing each word individually. This verse has always been a comfort to me regarding who God is—strength from within and a shield from attacks from without, therefore, I have a song in my heart. It became a life verse for me. All Northwestern students had Christian work assignments, which for me was largely singing or playing the piano in various churches. Others taught Sunday school, preached, or did youth ministry. Though this was extracurricular to our studies, it was a valuable part of our education.

Perhaps the greatest joy at Northwestern was traveling with the A Capella choir as we took a month-long tour each spring, which covered many miles in different directions of the United States. I also got to present several fifteen minute programs on our college radio station, KTIS.

Ready to leave on choir tour

After singing at our missions' conference in my freshman year, I was asked to make some recordings for two radio stations, HCJB in Ecuador and ELWA in Africa. God was already showing me that music could very much be used on the mission fields of the world. Each year we were introduced to many outstanding missionaries. Dr. Harry Stam, head of the Missions Department, had a great love for these people and instilled a desire for missions throughout the student body. The communist Chinese had beheaded his brother John and wife Betty Stam. As a result Dr. Stam had an undying passion for missions and was very influential in students' lives.

During a summer break from college, my mom's sister, Aunt Louise, was visiting us and looked through my yearbook. To my surprise she said she knew two of the students, Charlotte and Steve Sonmor. She had gone to college with their mother. Lo and behold, my mom also knew who they were as she had worked for their grandmother at one time. I knew Steve vaguely as he was in choir with me and I sometimes met him when we had gotten off from a city bus after our day's work. A bit shy, I always wondered what I would say to him since I had never officially met him. Not too long after learning this information from my aunt, my roommate and I were out ice-skating on the pond in Loring Park that more or less served as our campus. Steve happened to be out there and he skated with my roommate. He was a great skater and I thought they would make a real nice couple. When it was time to leave, he helped Marijo take off her skates and I guess he helped me also. I told him that I had an aunt that knew his mother as they had gone to school together. He asked me a bit about it. Back in our room I told Marijo he might be a nice guy for her. She agreed he was very nice.

The following evening after our meal in the school

cafeteria, Steve caught up with me and said, "Hey, tell me about this aunt of yours who knows my mom." I explained that my Aunt Louise had apparently gone to college with his mom. We talked about a lot of things like the Minnesota/Wisconsin football game going on that weekend. I told him it really didn't matter to me who won even though I live in Minnesota because I was born in Wisconsin. He of course wanted to know where I was born. I said, "It's such a small place with possibly nothing more than a gas station and a tavern; you've probably never heard of it." At his insistence, I told him it was Wilson, Wisconsin to which he replied, "That's where I live now. That's where I was born." I had heard he was from Luck, Wisconsin, so this surprised me. Apparently his family was in Luck when he started college but moved back to Wilson. We found out his birthplace and mine were just a half-mile apart.

The following evening he asked me to go to the valentine formal with him which was still several weeks away. I accepted but inwardly I was worried that Marijo might be hurt. Thankfully, she was just fine with it. Before the formal banquet took place, we had the annual missionary conference for the college with evening meetings being held in First Baptist Church of Minneapolis, not too many blocks from the college. Steve asked me if I would like to go with him, which involved walking, as very few college students had cars at that time.

We went out for a strawberry sundae in a quaint little shop before he brought me home. Then he did something no other guy had ever done on a date with me. He prayed with me at the door and then said goodnight. He was such a gentleman and very thoughtful. I really hadn't had time to decide what I thought of him as I hardly knew him. Yet even then, I had a strange feeling that this guy was who I was going to marry because of the many coincidences in our lives. Our families knew each other, our home churches were in the same fellowship of Conservative Baptist Churches, and we both had a love for music. He had considered the same three colleges I had contacted and God led us both to Northwestern.

We went to several meetings together during the conference and one of the nights there was a call for those to come forward that were willing to give their lives for missionary service if God should so lead. I never forgot the touch on my shoulder and my response to the Lord. I knew I had to be obedient. We both rose simultaneously and went forward. He explained that he always thought he would be a pastor but was beginning to see the greater need for missionaries.

One would think this would be a courtship made in heaven, and yes, I believe it was; yet there were many challenges. The fact that our families knew each other was not all "roses." Steve's family was not too thrilled about my mother's family background for various reasons, predominately dealing with health issues, so we had a rather "off and on" relationship for a while. I could write pages on this subject alone! This was very hurtful to me until I looked at it from the eyes of parents wanting the best for their son. When we were in one of those "off" times I looked up at him in the balcony where he sat in chapel. Everyone but Steve had left his or her seat and he alone was still seated and was looking down at me with a sad look in his eyes. *"What was he thinking?* I felt sure he cared for me and I knew how much I had come to care for him. He was a committed Christian and displayed leadership abilities. He served on student council, was president of his class, and president of the Student Missions Fellowship. I also noticed he was very disciplined in his work habits, and enjoyed music as I did.

Our high school graduation pictures

At one point in our relationship, Steve related his testimony regarding his salvation. He said at the age of thirteen, he was walking from the barn to the house one evening when he looked up to the sky and noticed an opening in the clouds. He thought, "What if the Lord should return tonight?" In his inner spirit he knew that if Christ did return, he would not be ready to go with Him, as he wasn't sure He was God's child. He felt as if God could open up the ground right there and swallow him into hell. God had his attention and he retreated to his room to read his Bible. However, nothing was very clear to him. A few days later, a young woman named Carol Archer came to the house announcing they were going to be having vacation Bible school in the church down in the valley where they attended, beginning the very next day. Though Steve was bothered about his relationship with God, he thought he was too old to go to Bible school. However, his mother said, "You're going." At the close of the session, the teacher explained the way of salvation and asked if anyone wanted to know for certain that they would go to heaven. If so, they were to raise their hand and she would deal with them afterwards. He and his younger sister, Faith, both accepted Christ that day. His parents had both received Christ in their adult years and were growing in the Lord and eager for their children to know for certain of their salvation.

Steve, after high school, worked on the Soo Line Railroad as a yard clerk. God really got hold of his life at that time. He would spend hours praying and reading the Word. He remembers that as a special time when the Lord dealt personally with him. He led a soul to Christ during that time and was excited about his faith and the prospect of serving Christ more fully. It was so much like my time prior to college when I began to seek deep cleansing in my life in preparation to serve the Lord. After one year out of high school, he came to Northwestern so he was a year and a half younger than I, which was better than most of my classmates who were at least two years younger.

Steve lost his thirteen year old sister, Faith, to cancer during his first year of college prior to my acquaintance with him. She had been a strong witness for the Lord in her short life. She died a very painful death with bone cancer. Her death greatly affected the entire family, so much so that they didn't want to stay in Luck, Wisconsin where Faith's death occurred. Steve graduated from Luck High School in 1952, and the family moved back to Wilson, Wisconsin—the area of their roots and mine. Their big farmhouse became a favorite place for the entire family in years to come. At the time the farmhouse was built, Sears Roebuck sold architectural house plans through their catalogue. The style of this house was one of their popular plans. Steve's grandparents purchased the plan in 1916. This is the home where Steve's father's large family of eleven siblings grew up.

The farmhouse

I know Faith's death had a very sobering effect on Steve and one day he told me he was afraid he had cancer as he had several lumps in various places on his body. I was devastated but insisted he go to our school doctor and at the same time, I prayed that God would keep me from worry and allow me to be able to concentrate on my schoolwork. God gave me peace in a marvelous way. I felt guilty for not worrying but God would not allow me to. What a marvelous manifestation of His grace. Steve returned from the doctor much relieved that those lumps were just a lot of fatty tumors that were nothing to worry about.

We both got involved in missionary prayer bands. By this time we had done some singing together. What a thrill it was to blend our soprano and tenor voices together. He wanted me to pray about what field God might be calling me to for missionary service. I agreed that I would and he would too. A few weeks later, after singing, "The Breaking of the Bread," he asked me if I had any idea yet where God would want me to go. I couldn't help but think, *what if God calls us to different fields?* Yet there was an underlying peace and I realized that God had consistently put the Philippines on my heart, through individuals and speakers. When I told him, he said that was true for him as well. He had been challenged by the testimony of the Denler twins, young men who served in the Philippines.

Another busy school year went by with choir tour and both of us involved in the "Voice of Christian Youth" radio broadcast. The next summer we were verbally engaged. I spent the summer on the east side of the Rocky Mountains with a travelling singing group for the college called "The Carolons." There were three girls and three guys. The three guys were a great trumpet trio and we sang in separate trios as well as a mixed sextet. Our ministry also included teaching and counseling at a camp, singing at Youth for Christ meetings and at various churches. Steve was working in an American Sunday School Union camp on the West side of the Rocky Mountains teaching and counseling. We were able to talk by phone on one occasion but were very eager to finally get back together again.

When I returned from Colorado, my family took a drive down to Wisconsin in the area of our birth and I said, "I just feel that Steve is right around here someplace." I knew he was supposed to be home soon. Then back in my dorm in Minneapolis, I said to my roommate, "I feel like Steve is going to walk in the door any minute." Immediately, yes immediately, there was a knock on the door and he was there. I told him about the feeling I had in Wisconsin that day and sure enough he had been there at his folks. Was that mental telepathy or wishful thinking? Only God knows.

During my junior year in college, Mr. Mogck asked me to participate in a contest for the vocal teachers of Minnesota. It was a preliminary contest, so some of the participants had to participate a second time at the Northrop Auditorium at the University of Minnesota. My good friend and partner with the Carolons group, Judy Jones, won the first time around. Not realizing this was still a contest, following my rendition of *If Thou Art Near (Bist du bei mir)* by J.S. Bach, I headed out the door. Suddenly someone was pulling me back, saying my name had been called as the first place winner in the finals. I was never so shocked. I can't recall the amount of the monetary prize, but I remember using that money to purchase Steve's wedding ring. God provided once again.

# Chapter 7

*Becoming One*

During our third year of college I really began to enjoy my studies and became more diligent and disciplined. I was privileged to have Dr. Stanley Toussaint for two Bible classes. He gave me a hunger for God's Word like I had never had before. I will always be grateful for this dear man of God.

Early in December Steve took me for a drive around one of the lakes in Minneapolis, and asked me if I was still willing to become his wife and prepare to go to the Philippines. After my affirmative answer, he removed my gloves and placed a diamond engagement ring on my finger. After our engagement, we began more ministry together in music and of course my mind was occupied with the wedding that was planned for August.

During that year we had the sadness of seeing my mom go through radiation treatments for cancer. This was heartbreaking to all of our family. However, she had recovered sufficiently to be a part of our wedding in August. We chose to get married in Steve's home church in Wisconsin rather than in Minneapolis where my family was then living. It was a difficult decision for me since I loved the beautiful new church in Minneapolis where the current pastor was the one who led me to Christ. However, as we considered all of the options, we realized that many of my mother's family and most of Steve's relatives from Wisconsin would perhaps not desire to drive to Minneapolis. Added to that, this little church had some special significance to my family as my father and grandfather had built the church as well as the pulpit furniture. It was the same little church, though in a new location, where my parents had played in their string band in the past. Winnifred Larson and her parents had a ministry there years before. Winnifred, known as "the Kate Smith of the Gospel," who often sang at Northwestern, was a close friend to my parents and Aunts, Hazel and Esther, in years past. She was a great contralto who knew how to sing with great feeling. My dad always encouraged me to sing like her.

We asked Rev. Herb Hazzard, State Youth Director of Minnesota Conservative Baptists, to officiate at our wedding, which took place August 3, 1957. Herb became very dear to us when I had been heavily involved in the state and Twin City Youth Activities. He had been a real encourager in my life during some difficult times. Herb was also a good photographer and managed to take our wedding pictures as well. Sadly, the man who was to develop them lost the negatives.

Having formerly worked in a florist shop, Steve's mother arranged all the flowers for the wedding as well as baking and decorating our wedding cake. She also made the candy mints with our names on each one. Her many talents included sewing, cooking, baking and arranging food and flowers beautifully.

It was necessary to evaluate everything on the basis of cost so we decided to sing to one another alternating solos on the verses of, "*Because*," as I walked up the aisle, and ending together in a duet on the final verse. Our prayer song was, "*Savior Like a Shepherd Lead us.*" My sister Hildi and Steve's sister Charlotte were our maid of honor and bridesmaid, respectively, and Steve's roommate, Leon Leeds, and my brother Ken, were Steve's attendants. Hildi sang a special arrangement of *"Bless This Home"* at the reception.

During the wedding, I overheard someone softly whimpering on my side of the auditorium and wondered who it was. Later, I discovered it was Aunt Esther, who had vowed not to come to the wedding. At the last minute she got a ride from some folks in Hastings and came after all. She was so afraid I would live a life of sorrow as so many women did and felt women got a raw deal in marriage. At the close of the wedding, however, she made the remark, "I've never seen so much love." I was so pleased that she came.

We had planned to use brother Ken's Chevrolet convertible on our honeymoon and he would use our old car for that week. However, Ken was not able to get our car started. Upon examination, we found someone had put water in the gas tank, likely as a wedding night prank, so this presented quite a dilemma. We weren't able to go to the pretty little place we had reserved for the night. We waited and waited at Steve's grandparents' home which was furnished but unoccupied at the time. It became the solution to our problem. My mom lovingly waited with me until Steve returned to be sure all was well. I knew she was extremely weary from her radiation treatments, yet she stayed with me. Now as a mom myself, I understand more of a mother's heart as I've seen our daughters move out from our nest. Steve's pastor, a young man from our college, offered us his new car to take on our honeymoon. (We had a sneaking suspicion he had something to do with the condition of our car, but who knows?).

We had a brief honeymoon in Northern Minnesota along the North Shore, as well as staying at a cabin near a lake in Northern Minnesota. Our cabin was designated as the honeymoon cabin so we received many comments and well wishes from people on the beach as we arrived. That night we heard a lot of noise on the roof and supposed it was the beach lovers having a little fun by throwing rocks. Upon checking, however, we found it was simply acorns falling from the tree above our cabin.

I smile when I realize that we came to the cabin that night in our "going away" clothes. I wore a pink jacket dress, pink heels, a matching broad brim pink hat and gloves. Steve wore a suit and tie! Those were the days when such was the wedding protocol. As you can imagine, this was not too practical, but we thought we had to do things properly.

Following the honeymoon, we headed back to what would be our first home together. It was an upstairs apartment in a house, not too far from college. Our first night in our apartment was very memorable. A young guy who worked with Steve came to visit us bringing a wedding gift, which was a picture of Christ. He said he really came to ask a question. He had observed Steve at work and wondered why Steve was so different from others. The young man mentioned worldly things Steve did not partake of. Steve was able to explain how Christ had changed his life. He decided that's what he wanted and Steve led him to Christ that night. He became a dear friend for many years. What a great memory of that first night in our first home together.

Us with attendants

Us with Parents

# Chapter 8

## *Graduation in Absentia*

As we moved into our senior year of college together, we were so busy we saw each other only briefly each day. We had lunch together at noon, choir practice on a few days a week and finally at night we were together. However, we worked at the same insurance company, Steve doing janitorial service while I worked in a stenographic pool. Occasionally we'd get a peek at each other when he walked by my office door.

While working at Northwestern National Life Insurance Company, I began to notice my vision was getting pretty strained after all of the close work. So I began to pray that God would supply the need for glasses. We were able to go on our last choir tour together and stayed in the home of a family who had members on several mission fields of the world. They were thrilled that we were planning to be missionaries and gave us a gift of money as we left their home. This was a significant amount that we used to supply the glasses I needed. With deepest thanks, I asked God to not allow them to get broken and I was very careful with them because He had provided them. Little did I know there would be a definite answer to that prayer.

Hildi wanted to purchase a new dress for me for graduation. Together we shopped in downtown

Minneapolis but never did find anything appropriate. Eventually we decided to give up on this venture and parted ways. On the way home to our apartment, at the intersection two doors down from our house, I stood and waited. There were no signal lights at that time, so I waited until the traffic slowed and was moving in the direction for me to cross. However, as I was almost across the street, I felt the impact of what proved to be a large Oldsmobile convertible going at full speed. I realized a car had hit me and that I was rolling on the pavement.

Meanwhile, Steve, concerned that I wasn't home yet, came out of our house in his stocking feet and observed the entire episode. Bending over me, he said to the officer, "This happens to be my wife!" I quickly said, "Honey, I'm okay." As I spoke, my mouth felt strange and I said, "I think my teeth are gone." He assured me, two teeth were simply chipped. The attending policeman said to Steve, "You are fortunate she is alive, most of them die after being thrown forty feet." Then someone found my glasses. They had apparently landed in the soft grass next to the sidewalk without a scratch. I was suddenly reminded of my prayer that they would never get broken. God was once again faithful in answering my prayer. Soon an ambulance arrived and I was loaded into it. I believe Steve rushed back to the house to get his shoes and his Bible and rode with me to Minneapolis General Hospital as he read the entirety of Romans 8 and said it took on a new meaning for him ever since.

At the hospital, doctors examined me and a nurse scrubbed my wounds. One doctor told me that my big toe was dislocated and my pelvis bone was cracked. Several doctors and interns tried to get my toe back in place by pulling on it. This produced excruciating pain like I had never experienced before. They soon discovered that each of my toes had shifted into the next one's position and it could only be corrected through surgery, far more serious than a break.

The following day I was given a spinal block, had the surgery, and was fitted with a cast up to my knee. I was not able to wear the cast very long as it rubbed on a large wound on my inner ankle. The pain of dislocation, worse than anything I had previously endured, reminded me of the Scripture in Psalm 22:14 NIV. It speaks prophetically of Jesus' death, "I am poured out like water, and all of my bones are out of joint." It made me identify more fully with the pain He must have endured.

I can't remember how long I was hospitalized, perhaps about two weeks. Many friends visited me including the man who caused the accident. He seemed truly sorry that he had caused me so much pain. I was thankful for his attitude and the acknowledgement of his carelessness.

It was disappointing not to be able to go through college graduation exercises. However, I attended Baccalaureate prior to the accident, and was selected to sing for our class. Since our college had a radio station, I heard the Commencement program on the radio there in the hospital. When my name was called to receive my diploma, they stopped and prayed for me. It made me feel a small part of the special time even in absentia. My family gathered at Hildi's place in honor of Steve's graduation that night though I couldn't be there.

Because the nurses heard my degree was in music, they thought I should go around to other wards and sing hymns to people to try to comfort and cheer them. I tried to decline, but they insisted. So here I was in a wheel chair with two black eyes, singing with no accompaniment, hymns that people either requested, or I chose. I felt very awkward doing this but the nurses insisted on it and I guess I will never know how God might have used it. I am reminded today of the great value of the hymns that most people pay little attention to anymore.

When I got out of the hospital, my dear mother came over to our apartment to try to help me with ironing. It was quite a distance for her to come by bus as they lived in south Minneapolis and we were on the north side. I knew she was still quite weak after her cancer treatments but she was always so willing to give of herself for others. I'm sure it was her way to show her love for me.

Following graduation, we both wondered what the next step was to be in our lives. We had prayed much for God's direction. Three possibilities presented themselves: (1 An invitation to pastor a church in Colorado, (2 begin a missionary internship program, or (3 go to seminary. I had hoped the Lord would lead Steve to attend Dallas Theological Seminary as I so appreciated the teaching of those who graduated from there. Steve agreed, but was getting weary of school and didn't know if he could begin studying again without a break. However one day while at work he felt God say that He wanted Him at Dallas Seminary. It was already getting close to the beginning of the school year but he sent his application in obedience to the Lord.

In the meantime our dear college friends, Rich Siemens and Gracie Megert had asked if we could be a part of their wedding in Oklahoma. We knew we could perhaps do it if we were going to Dallas, but Steve had not yet gotten his acceptance so we didn't know what to tell them. We decided to give up our apartment as we felt surely we would be doing one of the three options. Then we heard that the church in Colorado was no longer an option as the pastor decided to stay on. The missionary internship was not in line with our church background so that was no longer a viable option. We still had no word from Dallas. Finally Steve called the seminary and found they had just mailed his acceptance that day. Once again God was faithful. Sometimes He tests us and makes us wait but when we truly seek His will, He makes it known. We were able to tell Rich and Gracie we would be a part of their wedding. They were going on to Dallas Seminary as well and eventually became missionaries to the Ivory Coast and later to Zambia and we've continued to be close friends.

# Chapter 9

⌘

## *Heartbreaking News*

Soon God put us through another trying time. We learned my mom's cancer was back and we found it very difficult to leave for Dallas as she was going in for more treatments. It was a tearful goodbye but we assured my family, if need be, we would return; but Steve had to get registered and we had to find an apartment in Dallas. It was with a very heavy heart that we left for Oklahoma and then to Dallas.

Upon our arrival in Dallas we knew we first had to find a place to live. It was about 106 degrees with 90 plus humidity when we were looking for an apartment and nothing appealed to us. We didn't want to be a burden to the Widders, our friends from college, who were now already at the seminary and had graciously let us stay with them. After reading in my devotions, "Withdraw thy foot from thy neighbor's house; lest he weary of thee, and so hate thee" (Proverbs 25:17 KJV), I prayed that God would help us find a place soon.

We visited a church that weekend and heard someone asking if anyone knew someone who needed an apartment. It was in a four-plex, furnished and air-conditioned for only $55 a month. Believe me, we were interested. The next day we met the owner who became our lovely landlady for the four years we were at Dallas. We loved our apartment, with gardenias and roses blooming in the front yard and our own carport and clothesline in the back. This dear Mrs. Grace owned the entire corner and almost all of her renters were seminary students. Again God knew just what we needed. We moved in the following day.

Next on the agenda was to find a job. I was now going to be the chief breadwinner, as we knew seminary was more than full time work for Steve. I found it a bit difficult applying to various offices as they would always comment, "Oh, so you're a Yankee." I never dreamed I would encounter those attitudes but it was very prevalent there. I found that I was expected to really dress up to apply for a job. My foot was still bothering me so I could only wear shoes with a slight high heel and I heard it was a "must" to wear a hat! What a time I had but I was able to land a good job at a cotton company that had outreaches all over the world. I was secretary to two of the overseas salesmen.

We had just barely gotten settled in our apartment and I'd found a job when we got word that Mom was not expected to live. She had written a letter herself telling us there was nothing more the doctors could do. We packed up and headed back to Minnesota where we quickly went to visit Mom at University Hospital. Our Pastor had been asked to break the news to Mom but when he came to see her she was able to tell him herself. God had given her a great calm and peace in her heart. I was amazed that the day before she passed away, she had gotten up and washed her own hair. I will always remember her last words to me: "I always wished I could do something like you are doing like going to a mission field." I told her she had been the best mom in the world. I could never have asked for anything better and that she had done what God called her to do.

After that day's visit, I hoped to come back the next day and just be with Mom to hold her hand and wait till she slipped into eternity. The following day we arrived and found we were too late. Hildi had been there with her for which I was so thankful. Glady and Ken came but Daddy was nowhere in sight. Glady and her then boyfriend went to find him in a bar to let him know that Mom had passed away that morning. This is one of my most difficult memories, though I suppose he was grieving in his own way.

I have never cried so much in my life as I did at Mom's funeral. I thought of all of the abuse she suffered, the hard work she went through often trying to balance two huge bags of groceries, one in each arm as she trudged through the snow after work. There were all of the arguments and demands upon her to get up and prepare my dad a meal at 1:00 or 2:00 o'clock in the morning, even though she had to get up and go to work in a factory and he was not working at all. Hildi and I would lie in bed where I would listen in case Mom needed help, and Hildi would cover up her head hoping she could block it out. We all had our own ways of coping with these difficulties.

After Mom's death I was concerned for Ken and Glady still so young without any parental care. Dad went to live in his own apartment. A former boss of mine came to our aid when she and her husband took both Ken and Glady into their home until they could get on their feet and move in with roommates. Glady had just graduated from high school that year. I knew it was not going to be easy to leave any of my precious family. Hildi was the stabilizing force in spite of her heart condition and though still single, she had her own room in a home, a good job, and did her best to look after our fragmented family.

At the funeral my thoughts were mostly consumed with my own failures. I had started sewing a dress for Mom and never finished it. I wanted to do so many things in an attempt to brighten her life and I had always seemed to be too busy with my own. I was reminded that my mom never owned a pair of earrings until my wedding day. Any jewelry she had was handed down from someone. She had a simple wedding band at one time but lost it, so we purchased a simple sterling silver band for her to wear. I wondered how God could ever forgive me when He had been so gracious to give me such a loving, sweet mom whose life was lived for Christ and her family. Oh, how much I still had to learn! I wondered how God was going to use the next step in my life to be a seminary wife and secretary in Dallas, Texas, in preparation for the day when we would sail off to the Philippines.

# Chapter 10

## *Seminary Years*

### 1958-1962

The next step in God's preparation for our lives as missionaries was now upon us. How grateful we were that we had our apartment and Steve's registration completed prior to Mom's death. I was thankful too that I had a job at the Cotton Company where I worked for the better part of a year. However, eventually we got word that most of the company was going to close for lack of funds so I had to trust the Lord for another job. Once again God was faithful. He always knows our needs even before we ask. Dr. Toussaint was now teaching at the seminary and his wife, Maxine, had known of a man for whom she had worked at Magnolia Oil and recommended me for a position there.

Since I had secretarial experience in both shorthand and typing, they assigned me to the most difficult man in the steno pool. The pay was good but I found it difficult to work for this man who did everything the long way, loving to dictate every letter rather than using form letters as all the other salesmen did. Then too, he had both wholesale and retail accounts so there was twice the volume of work. I could never leave work with a clean desk as the other girls did. I also resented being called "Monroe," the name he bestowed on me, every time he wanted to dictate a letter. In general, his language was an offense to me yet God had put me there for that time and season. Steve found if we went home for that summer, he could work at Ceco steel where he had previously worked. That would help take care of tuition costs and enable us to get away from the heat of the Texas summer. Working for this salesman was getting more frustrating by the day and I realized I could not keep it up. We felt God was telling us that I should leave the job and trust the Lord. We then found that the principal of Dallas Christian Grade School, also a seminary student, needed an apartment just for the summer. It worked out perfectly for that period of time, so that our apartment was reserved for us.

Soon the school year was again upon us. While contemplating where to apply for work, another seminary wife called inquiring if I would be interested in teaching physical education at Mesquite High School, a suburb of Dallas. She had already begun teaching in that position but was actually trained to be an elementary teacher and had found a job available to her. She felt sure if they would take her they would accept me. I was not trained in physical education though I loved it in high school. I was prepared to be a music teacher. She also mentioned that the superintendent was a Christian and he really wanted Christian teachers. Although a bit dubious I decided to give it a try. *Maybe this is what God has in store for me.* A ride had already been worked out a with another seminary wife. Praise God, I was given the job. What a joy to work in a school where Scripture and student-led prayers were offered each morning over the public address system. The Lord enabled me to be a witness to many of the girls in my classes and many of them who were Christians came to me for counsel and encouragement. I especially enjoyed the track and field sports during the spring season when we could enjoy the great outdoors. God also allowed me to use my music in playing hymns for a history pageant presented by that department. I was asked to come back the following year but since I was just there provisionally, I would need to take additional courses in order to keep the job.

At the end of the school year we got a call from a camp in Wyoming asking if we would consider spending our summer as camp missionaries. It seems they had difficulty getting experienced missionaries so they were willing to take us since our intent was to eventually get there. Steve, being the outdoorsman that he is, really wanted to do this and we prayed much, for it meant I would have to get another job in the fall. We also had to pay for our apartment if we wanted to keep it. *"Lord"*, we prayed, *"What do you really desire of us at this time?"* He then provided Steve with an opportunity to work for our landlady that paid for our apartment for the summer months.

While in Wyoming, I received a call concerning a job for the coming year. I was asked to teach elementary music at Dallas Christian Grade School; also to teach Music Fundamentals, direct a girls' choir and teach voice at Dallas Bible Institute only a few blocks from the seminary. We again marveled at God's provision. "It shall come to pass That before they call, I will answer" (Isaiah 65:24a).

Never did I ever dream I would be able to do the very thing I always wanted to do. Steve also had the privilege of teaching physical education to the boys at the grade school. I had the joy of writing a Christmas program for the school that would involve every student. It was held at Scofield Memorial Church, a lovely old church with stained glass windows. The decor fit the theme of the program perfectly. Little did I know my program would one day be translated into Tagalog and used in two churches in the Philippines and again in a stateside church.

The students at the Bible institute were such a blessing to us. Some of them attended the same church we did and would meet at our home for prayer meeting on Wednesday night as it was too far for all of us to drive out to the church in Duncanville. I had two Guatemalan students for voice who had a similar background to that of the Filipinos I would someday teach and they became very special to me.

Following the school year of 1960 we again got a call to go to Wyoming and work in a church as well as the camp. We were thrilled to go there again but needed to find a way to keep our apartment. Mrs. Grace, our landlady, graciously said we could keep it if Steve could do certain repairs for her before and after our summer ministry. Once again we were able to serve the Lord in Camp Bethel near Sheridan, Wyoming, as well as the First Baptist Church in Powell. I directed the choir occasionally and we both got to do some teaching. It was a joy to get to know many of the young people personally and to keep in touch with them through the years. Pastors in Wyoming and Montana became well known to us and later were good contacts for our missionary endeavors.

# Chapter 11

*Great Expectations*

We had a big surprise, however, as the summer ended. We suspected new life was budding within me and wondered, if so, what would happen regarding my job. We made it known to the elementary principal and the chairman of the music department of the Bible Institute and each decided I would just teach for the first semester since the birth was to be in April.

That Christmas we went home as usual. Steve's mom, in particular, became suspicious that I was carrying more than one baby. Because it was my first pregnancy, I didn't know what to expect. However, we began to notice a lot of movement and I was wider than usual. I thought perhaps it was just because I was short. However, we remembered that Sears had a plan in their catalogue if one ordered a complete layette for a baby and later had twins, they would provide a second free layette. Since we had wondered about twins but did not yet know for sure we took advantage of that offer.

Our next-door neighbors, Larry and Virginia Oubre, also in seminary, had twin girls now about a year old. We had the same doctor so of course we compared notes. Virginia had several miscarriages before her twins were born so the doctor didn't even tell her she was going to have twins for fear she would be very distraught and lose them. She told me he might let me know if I didn't seem worried. At my next doctor's appointment, I ventured out and said, "My husband thinks we're going to have twins, but that is probably too good to be true." Steve had already been praying for "the babies" every day. The doctor then told me, "I knew from your first visit that you were going to have twins as I could hear two heartbeats but I didn't want to alarm you."

We were overjoyed! Hadn't I always made my paper dolls into twins? Then we began to realize the cost involved. Two bassinets, two cribs, two high chairs, two infant seats, two sets of clothing and diapers! *"Oh, God,"* we prayed, *"We don't know how these needs are going to be met but we know you are in control."* Each morning in my devotions, I would pray for good temperaments and that they would be good little babies who would be healthy and grow up to know and love Him.

Another issue kept us guessing. Would it be two boys, two girls or a boy and a girl? Only God knew. We would accept whatever God gave us. Steve of course was hoping for at least one boy so I had ordered the first layette in blue. Eventually my doctor wanted me to have an X-ray to determine the babies' positions. There were no ultrasounds at that time of course, but it was exciting to see two tiny forms with heads downward. I was a bit concerned that I couldn't see any arms or legs but the doctor said not to worry, they didn't always show up but they are there. He thought they would be close to four pounds each at that point. Little did I know that the very next day they would be born. April 6th would have been their due date, but they arrived March 7, 1961. Fortunately, Steve had been prompted to take out health insurance enough in advance so that all expenses were taken care of for their birth. That week was the seminary's annual missionary conference, which meant no classes or homework for Steve. He was able to be with me in the labor room as the doctor marked two red X's where he heard the heartbeats; then off to the delivery room I went. I was given no anesthesia other than gas at the moment of the birth due to the fact that the babies were so small. The first words of significance I heard in the delivery room were, "Well, here's the second one already—another little girl." It was then I heard a piercing cry. I knew then that we had girls and gave the names we had chosen, Tamara [Tami] Lynn for the first one and Terri Lee born four minutes later. They looked so very tiny and I felt some regret that I couldn't do a better job. That night around midnight the pediatrician came in and woke me to tell me that though they were very small, Tami, 3 pounds 11 ounces, and Terri at 3 pounds 9 ounces, he assured me they were very healthy. He said he knew I'd sleep better if I knew how they were doing. Never have I been so excited and thrilled. Their newborn cries were like a symphony to my ears and truly God had given me the desire of my heart.

In that day, we were not allowed to touch our premature infants until they weighed 5 pounds and we could bring them home. It was heart breaking to come every day to the hospital and look helplessly through the glass of their incubators, unable to help them when they cried or got into an awkward position. We called the nursery each day to get a record of their weight and a loss of even an ounce or so always brought concern.

Finally the day came when we brought Tami home. I recall it was on Good Friday. I cherished holding her and didn't want to put her down. I only felt sad that Terri was still at the hospital. Steve's mom had come from Wisconsin to be with us when they came home. I was forever grateful as Tami cried all night long and we discovered it was due to constipation. Grandma ended up having to give her an enema. I didn't know how to give an enema and especially to one so tiny. I also had to get up early on Easter Sunday to sing in an Easter program in one of the professor's churches. I had a high soprano solo and I know only the Lord gave me strength to do it.

Tami eventually began to adjust, but we had a repeat performance when Terri came home on Easter Monday. I'm sure after a month in the hospital they had much to adjust to at home. The girls had to be fed every two hours and because they ate very slowly we would just get done with one and we'd have to feed the other one. We loved them so but we were absolutely exhausted. In time we resorted to bottle holders and sat with them when they ate to be close to them. This enabled both to eat at once and develop a better schedule for them and us. However, one day Grandma Sonmor got them confused and put them in the wrong bassinets so I ended up feeding Terri twice and letting Tami go hungry! They were difficult to keep straight so we kept a birth bracelet on one of them until she outgrew it. We were told they were fraternal twins, however, doctors who have treated them since, say they have to be identical. I know there are many differing theories on how twins are formed and in the final analysis, it is the Lord's design.

Steve with Tami, Marilyn with Terri

Grandma and Grandpa Sonmor with twins

I could write a great deal about the adventure of having twins and the fun they had when they discovered each other, stole each other's pacifiers and giggled together in their playpen but that is not the purpose for this book. Predominately, my aim is to share God's faithfulness through the everyday affairs of life. Needless to say, they have brought us abundant joy to this day.

During the last summer we would be in Dallas, my sister, Hildi, married Bill Mann, a fine Christian young man from Princeton, Minnesota. Things worked out for us to go back to Minnesota for her wedding where I was maid of honor and sang. Steve was a groomsman. Steve went back to his old job at Ceco Steel and we stayed with his folks.

We were concerned that the girls were still not gaining weight like we thought they should. They had to be on a diet formula, as they couldn't tolerate the fat in most baby formulas. We prayed that we would know what was best for them. I began reading Dr. Spock's baby book, the only medical book I had, and found that if babies couldn't tolerate formula, it would be wise to try homogenized milk in which the fats are more evenly distributed. I decided to try it and they no longer had the constant diarrhea and began to gain weight. When we got back to Dallas our pediatrician was glad for the choice I had made. We were so grateful to have Christian doctors through this whole event.

That year with two little girls crawling and getting into everything we knew it would be difficult to make the trip home for Christmas. Therefore, we stayed in Dallas and enjoyed our own little family. A flocked pink Christmas tree was purchased and decorated with pink lights and balls. We carefully placed it on a table where little eyes could see but little fingers could not touch.

Again God provided for us, as I taught part time the last semester. The seminary had no classes on Mondays and the Bible College arranged my classes to be on that day when Steve could be home with the twins. God continued to provide our every need. Bassinets, cribs, high chairs and all those needs were provided. Sometimes a delivery truck would come to our door and we had no idea who sent the various items. Other seminary families loaned things to us. My neighbor who had the twins let me use her twin stroller, as her girls were old enough that they no longer needed it. God amazingly supplied everything we needed through those years.

Not only did God supply our needs, He provided many opportunities to serve Him. We sang in various churches, cantatas, and seminary events. I was also able to get in on some free classes for wives. One was with Howard Hendricks and another was with Dorothy Pentecost. We met in her home each week where she gave us notes that she eventually included in her book, *The Pastor's Wife*.

How blessed we were. We were privileged to hear many special lecturers each year at the seminary. I will always remember when Rachel Saint, sister of Nate Saint, one of the five martyrs in Ecuador, brought Dyuma, an Auca tribeswoman to share her testimony. I found it strange that she became very ill from the common cold. She had never had a cold until she entered the U.S. It taught us that there would be unexpected conditions in foreign lands and cultures.

The seminary had a great weekly fellowship for wives where we had various types of programs and special speakers. I served in three positions in that organization which taught me much concerning organization and administration. That experience would prove very beneficial in future years with women's ministry in the Philippines.

During our time in Dallas, all of Steve's family and several of mine visited us. Aunt Hazel came after the twins were born, as well as my sister Hildi prior to her marriage. Ken came once but I don't recall Glady being able to come. She was then at Northwestern College seeking to get ready for her recitals and subsequent graduation. We were blessed to have several friends from our college days attend Dallas and we had wonderful fellowship, often gathering in one of our homes for Thanksgiving.

God graciously gave us Mrs. Grace, a godly landlady who cared for us like a mother. When any illness struck, she was quick to bring us a cup of sassafras tea to speed us on to better health. To this day, Tami and Terri have the beautifully decorated Christmas stockings she made for them as babies. Each year they continue to be a part of their Christmas home decor.

Our lives are richer because of those four years in seminary not only for the Biblical knowledge and ministry preparation, but also for the friendships made, opportunities to serve, and the many things He taught us about trusting in Him. We kept in touch with Mrs.

Grace while in the Philippines and shortly before her death she and her daughter sent us a tape recording. God will reward her for her many kindnesses to us.

Before we knew it, graduation came. I was so thankful that typing papers for Steve until the wee hours of the morning had ended; however, I didn't know there would be more of them in the future. There was a ceremony for the wives as well. Mrs. Walvoord, the wife of the seminary president, presented each of the wives with a PHT diploma for "putting hubby through". I had to speak on behalf of the wives, as I was the president that year. I shared how God had led us to Dallas and hopefully to our ultimate goal, the Philippines.

Steve's family came for his graduation and we took a trip down to Galveston and Houston, an area so beautiful in the springtime. Many things were new to us Midwesterners, such as dogwood trees, redbud trees, and azaleas. Hildi and Bill came for graduation and took some of our things in their trailer and the rest we loaded into the trailer built by my brother-in-law Bill and brother Ken. We stayed with Steve's folks in Minneapolis for a while and later with Hildi and Bill for most of that summer. Steve returned to his old job at Ceco Steel for the summer while we waited upon the Lord for the next step. The twins were now walking and talking and I had the joy of being home with them.

# Chapter 12

## *Greenwood*

It was 1962 and seminary was behind us, we wondered what our next step would be. We knew God had called us to plant churches, therefore, Steve felt we should have some experience in a pastorate here in the states. This was not going to be easy for we would have to make plain our eventual plans to any church that considered us.

God had His plan, however, and led us to the Missionary Baptist Church in Greenwood, Wisconsin, in the heart of the dairy land. The church truly lived up to its name agreeing to take us even for a short time. We were not immediately thrilled about it, however, as the parsonage was an apartment above the church. It had only one entrance, which was a stairway from the front door of the church to the upstairs apartment. They eventually built a stairway leading to the backyard, which helped a great deal. Steve was asked if he would mow the lawn. He said he would, though it was about an acre in size with quite a bit of it on a side hill and didn't make for easy mowing. The salary was $50 a week, however, the people often supplemented our food supply with butter, milk, eggs, and other commodities. We were thankful we had no car payment to contend with so we managed to get by.

Missionary Baptist Church, Greenwood, Wisconsin

Steve had a weekly radio broadcast at a neighboring town. It was a very short program on Sunday mornings called "Moment of Truth." I remember how excited Tami and Terri were as they sat in their high chairs and heard their daddy on the radio. "Dadeeeeee" they would shout over and over again. Occasionally I was able to go with him and present music if we happened to have someone to stay with the girls.

Thanks to Aunt Hazel, who many years before, taught me to sew, I made my own clothes. Our family had what I call "a common thread," since my great grandfather came from Sweden to Minneapolis as a tailor. One of his sons was the only tailor in my hometown and Aunt Hazel did altering for the main department store there. It was very common to sew our own clothes when I was growing up. Our family also supplied us with clothes at times. We were about 120 miles from the Twin Cities where most of the family lived so they managed to visit us occasionally and we were together for most holidays. God blessed us in so many ways through these days.

We had a fine group of young people in the church. I was especially grateful for the two teenage girls, Pat Richardson and Beth Schrimper, who were our chief baby sitters who also cared for the twins during the church services whenever I had to play the piano. We had no church nursery so each of them would hold one of the girls. No one else seemed to see the need for a nursery but I have to say most parents did pretty well to keep their little ones quiet. I worked hard at teaching the girls to whisper and they always brought their New Testaments and a pad of paper and a pencil to keep them occupied. Terri particularly wanted her "Bibo" with her continually and would take it in the car or wherever we went. If she happened to get an "owie" she would cry and say, "I want my Bibo." She even wanted to sleep with it. Soon her little testament got worn out. We decided to give her a little address book the size of the New Testament and she was content with that. However, while in a store in a neighboring town one day, she happened to lay it down and leave it behind. Big tears flowed as she said; "I left my Bibo in that store." We had to go back and retrieve the prized little address book. I often think of that when I get down and discouraged. I too run to my Bible, which is my daily comfort and guide.

We had a couple of scares with Terri: One was when she got a piece of candy caught in her throat and began to choke. I told the girls that particular candy was a "no no," and placed it up high but I guess that made it more desirable! I immediately grabbed her and held her by her feet and pounded on her back as the candy fell to the floor. Tami's reaction was, "Mommy, why did you spank Terri when she was crying?" It took some explaining of course. Another time she fell out of her crib and seemed to be stiff as I picked her up. We were afraid of a concussion and rushed to the nearest hospital but found she was okay. Most of the trauma was in Tami's life, as you will see later, however, Terri had her share of it now and then. Often when Terri was fearful in the night, she would climb out of her crib and come quietly and sleep on the rug next to our bed so she'd be closer to us. It was a surprise to waken in the morning with a soft little bundle on the floor!

Bedtime was always a fun time

We had many and varied activities with the youth of the church. On one occasion they put on a banquet for the adults presenting a program with yesteryear in mind. At another banquet, we invited a speaker from Northwestern College along with a girls' trio to present the music. The speaker had formerly been with the Mafia and had a great testimony. My sister Glady was a member of the trio. Glancing down the table at Glady I noticed an extra big smile on her face. It was then I noticed the diamond ring on her finger. She was so happy to surprise me.

That year after her graduation, she married Tom Mix, an exceptionally bright young man who graduated with honors in all levels of his education. He had become a teaching fellow at Northwestern at this time. We were so happy for them. Hildi was maid of honor and I was a bridesmaid and soloist at Tom and Glady's wedding. I sewed my dress as well as Hildi's. At one point I got so frustrated with something that wasn't working out on the dress. I think it was button loops or something difficult to manage. I was at the point of tears when my dear mother-in-law noticed my dilemma and offered to help me. I had not been feeling up to par and wasn't aware of why I was so upset. The day after we got back from the wedding, I discovered I was having a miscarriage and was rushed to the neighboring town where I was hospitalized.

While we were at Greenwood, we made application to our mission board, which was then called Conservative Baptist Foreign Mission Society. The headquarters were in Wheaton, Illinois. Today the mission is called World Venture and is located in Littleton, Colorado. It was difficult to leave the twins as we set out for Wheaton, particularly because they had high fevers when we left them. They were staying with Grandma and Grandpa Sonmor, and Steve's sisters, Charlotte and Phoebe. I fought the tears all the way from Minneapolis to the middle of Wisconsin. Upon arriving in Wheaton, we of course called the folks for an update and got even more concerned as we found the twins had the red measles. In spite of troubles on the home front, we met with the Board and had extensive medical and psychological examinations. We also had to work at the Wheaton office for two weeks to be observed by the board and staff to determine our work ethics and how we behaved in general.

I recall an unpleasant incident of being falsely accused by a prominent mission official, of coming to breakfast with my hair up in curlers. The problem was I didn't even own any curlers, as my hair is naturally curly, yet the one who accused me would not back down. It was a painful experience but I had to just shake it off. However, it was a good preparation for the mission field and life in general as there are always times we have to just grin and bear unjust criticisms.

Our Commissioning Service for CBFMS

While we were in Greenwood, we got acquainted with Don and Mary Lou Decker who owned one of the two grocery stores in town. They had twin boys a bit older than our girls. They invited us for dinner one night and Steve presented the way of salvation to which Mary Lou responded that night. Later we had them at our home and Don also made a decision for the Lord. He gave Steve a ride in his plane and we became good friends though they were attending another church in town. Don passed away some years ago and Mary Lou married a widower from our church. We recently got a precious letter from her explaining how every child and grandchild in the family now knows the Lord. What a blessing to see their testimony still spreading out to others.

Steve was ordained during our last year in Greenwood. It was a joy to have so many friends and relatives join us for the occasion. In the year and three months we ministered in Greenwood, God gave us thirty-two people who followed the Lord in baptism.

The church allowed us to make a few trips for deputation but we did not really begin until after we left the church. Prior to our departure, the church hosted our commissioning service for the mission field with many pastors in the area. Our mission's area representatives Warren and Mable Steward presented music. We gave our testimonies concerning our call and sang a duet. Because we were bidding goodbye to the church, many people were crying. Tami and Terri had been sitting quietly on the front row, however, when people started crying they became a bit alarmed. They didn't cry but simply got up and joined us on the platform each one holding one of our hands as we continued our song. It was precious to us as well as the church.

The Richardson family and many others were so faithful to us even after we left. One young man from our youth group took on some of our support and Earl and Rachel Richardson and children, Pat and Brent, took on the responsibility of sending out our prayer letters. God knew what we needed when he placed us in Greenwood though it was but a short time.

Earl and Rachel Richardson

# Chapter 13

─────── ⁂ ───────

# *Our Most Memorable Christmas*

We had become so attached to the people in Greenwood that it was difficult to leave them. However, we had to find another temporary home while we engaged in our missionary deputation. A pastor-friend from college knew our need and informed us of a little house available rent-free. A widow in Baldwin, Wisconsin, wanted to move to be nearer her relatives after her husband's death and was willing to allow a Christian family to live in her home while she was gone. The timing seemed right as well as the price. Baldwin was not too far from the Twin Cities so access to travel facilities, when needed, would be good and it would not be too far from our families. Steve's first cousin, Keith Albrightson lived across the street.

Steve and some friends hauled our belongings to the house and the twins and I followed. I will never forget that depressing night as we looked at the room that was to be Steve's office. All of the bathroom aids for the man who died were still there and many things had to be taken out and stored. I had never seen so many black leather rocking chairs in one place before! As I recall, Steve and I slept on a stack of mattresses and the twins not far from us were crying, "Mommy, we can't reach you." The surroundings were anything but pleasant and familiar. However, they were brave little girls and soon settled down. I came close to tears as well but decided to laugh instead and make it an adventure, which it truly was.

Exploring the house a bit further the next day, we realized the bathroom had a sink and toilet but no bathtub. Since the owner was not averse to improvements we sought to find a bathtub and a friend, Joe Menter, helped get it installed. Gradually, we somehow transformed the place and it was a bit more like home. I never quite got used to having a water heater in the kitchen but we found we could get used to that too.

Things were going quite smoothly till one day we were in for a big surprise when I found that I had symptoms of another pregnancy. We had planned to wait until we got to the Philippines but God knew best. Therefore, travel for me and the twins was somewhat curtailed. We were thrilled at how God supplied our needs with fifty-two churches plus some individuals who had taken on our support. They were located from the east to the west and from Texas to Northern Minnesota. Later we added a church in Honolulu, Hawaii. Needless to say we knew our furloughs would be very busy in the future.

Steve travelled a great deal. When the distance wasn't too great, the twins and I would accompany him. Occasionally he would have to fly as a great amount of our support came from the eastern states. When he was gone for a length of time, the girls and I would go and stay with one of our relatives in the Twin Cities or Hastings with Aunt Hazel. She was alone now after Aunt Esther had passed away during our time in seminary. Aunt Hazel was no longer working at the telephone company as dial phones had now been installed throughout the city. She had difficulty finding employment so she got a job doing alterations for the largest department store in town and took sewing into her home. Her funds were very limited. One day she couldn't find enough cash to pay a utility bill. She searched the house and found a little red purse that Glady had left there with a few pennies in it. However, she knew this belonged to Glady and there is no way she would take funds from that little savings in the purse even though she knew Glady would gladly have given it to her. She prayed and asked God to help her find a few more pennies in her house. She continued to look until she found them. I will always remember this incident as a great example of the integrity that characterized this woman's life. She was a precious gift to all of us.

On another of the occasions when we stayed with Aunt Hazel, we were having a family picnic. Tami now almost four years old reached up to the table for something and a pot of boiling hot coffee spilled all over her arm and leg. I immediately put her under cold water, saw the skin peel off, and rushed her to the hospital emergency room where she lay in ice for a while and later was wrapped in gauze bandages covered with Vaseline. It took a few months for healing but how we praise God that only one scar remained—a slight indentation on one thigh. That same summer we were speaking at a camp and met another child who had been burned with hot coffee and was badly scarred. How thankful we were for God's wonderful grace and mercy and also for my mother-in-law earlier telling me about using cold water immediately in the event of a burn.

Added to preparation for another baby, we had another hurdle to cross. As missionary appointees we were required to attend linguistic training at McGill University in Toronto, Canada. We were encouraged not to bring our children, but with the unsettled experiences we had gone through, we decided to bring them as we were told childcare would be provided. Tami and Terri were real troopers and became eager to go to the childcare each day. We thank God for the way they adjusted to all of the change in their lives. Everything worked out well other than the fact that I was battling tiredness and all-day nausea as I always did with a pregnancy. However, it turned out to be a good experience all in all as we met other missionaries and learned how to make various sounds which we had never made before. We also learned some cultural issues relating to various people groups.

In addition to the training, we met some fine people who entertained us royally while we were there. The assistant pastor of one of the churches asked us to minister in music on several occasions. We also visited other churches coming and going to Toronto. It was a special privilege to stay with my high school friend and neighbor, Bernice Kaser, who then lived in Ohio. I remember when she became a Christian and eventually married a pastor. I decorated her wedding cake and sang at her wedding. I'll never forget it as the organist's music flew out an open window as I was singing. Somehow we both made it through the song without a glitch.

As time went on we all became more anxious for this new little one. My sister, Hildi, sister-in-law, Loma, and cousin Pat were also expecting at the same time and that added to the excitement. Of course all of our family, especially Steve, wanted a little boy as he only had sisters. Sadly, Hildi lost her precious son a day or so after his birth. She had previously lost a daughter also. We felt so badly for her but upon examination, the doctor found she had a divided uterus in which the partition would not allow enough room for a baby to grow to full-term. At least the doctors knew how to correct it with surgery for which we were so thankful. Loma and Ken's little girl, Lynette, was born October 1ˢᵗ and today she and her family are missionaries in Romania. Cousin Pat also had a son, Clay.

Steve was speaking in Wisconsin Rapids the day I went into labor. The twins and I were at Pastor Hess' home for Sunday dinner that day and I knew labor was beginning. It really became a blessing as Tami and Terri could stay and play with their friends, the Hess children, and were so excited about being there that their minds were not troubled at all when I left them.

Early in the afternoon on December 13, 1964, I went to the hospital and labor continued into the next day. It was a difficult labor as the baby was in posterior position. Though Steve hurried home as fast as he could, he still had to wait for the birth. How grateful we were to have our boy! He had lots of dark hair and weighed 6 lbs. 5 oz. We named him Stephen Mark but decided to call him Mark since there were already two Steve's in the family. Soon it was time to bring him home and the twins were overwhelmed with joy, begging to feed him, change him etc. We were so blessed to have the birth here rather than in the Philippines and this added to the joy for our families to get to know him prior to our departure.

Perhaps the greatest memory we have of living in Baldwin was our last Christmas prior to leaving for the Philippines. We invited my entire family and Steve's immediate family for Christmas Eve.

While I was still in the hospital, Charlotte and Phoebe had decorated a lovely Norway pine tree, flocking it with artificial snow and adding the many decorations I had made beforehand. The twins were old enough to sing "Away in a Manger" which brought tears to everyone's eyes, knowing how much all of the family would miss them. The twins asked us that night if they would turn brown when they got to the Philippines! Mark was in the car seat under the Christmas tree along with Ken and Loma's little Lynette who had just been born 2 months earlier. We were reminded of God giving His only Son on behalf of the sins of the world. We already loved our only son so much and wondered how God the Father could give His only son for all mankind especially while we were yet sinners.

We had a huge winter blizzard that Christmas Eve and it wasn't safe for anyone to drive home that night. Fortunately, Hildi and Bill had the foresight to bring two folding cots in case of bad weather. We had purchased two bunk beds and a trundle bed to take to the Philippines. Mark slept in his car bed, giving his bassinette to little Lynette, and the twins went back to sleeping in their cribs. The men all slept downstairs on a studio couch and cots, the women upstairs on the new beds, but we had one problem. Where was Daddy going to sleep? He was not happy. He insisted, "I can't sleep anywhere but in my own bed. I just have to go home." Then we remembered there was a roll away bed on the back porch with a feather tick mattress, and we set it up for him in the kitchen. He realized then he had no choice and the next day told us, "That was the best sleep I've ever had." Truly the blizzard turned out to be a blessing in disguise. That night will always remain in our memories as one of our happiest Christmases when God's love poured out upon us. It was one that would never be repeated but was a memory to store in our hearts forever.

The twins adored their best Christmas present.

Twins singing "Away in a Manger"

# Chapter 14

_~m~_

## *Fire! Fire!*

Spring began to adorn the countryside and we got word that the widow wanted to return to her house in Baldwin. We still had a little more support to raise when, in the midst of our packing, we were uprooted again. A little cottage in the country owned by Steve's Aunt Mabel (his dad's sister) became available. It was not far from Baldwin. However, it had no running water or indoor plumbing. It was a cozy little place and the farm scenery around the area was beautiful. We had two inconveniences which were common to many farmers of that time—having to haul water and use an outhouse. We both grew up with situations like that but found we had gotten pretty accustomed to the more modern conveniences.

We did most of our packing while living there preparing to ship our goods to the West Coast. All was going well until the day Steve started burning some trash. A sudden wind came up and blew sparks onto the roof of a shed where we had stored the things to be shipped. He yelled, "Honey, come quick, the shed is on fire." He was inside frantically throwing things out as fast as he could. I was afraid he wouldn't get out in time. He said, "Quick, go to Aunt Mabel's and tell her the shed is burning and call the fire department." I dreaded driving our new Chevrolet carryall as I had never driven a vehicle of that size and

I surely didn't look forward to informing Aunt Mabel her shed was burning. Since there was no choice, off I went despite my fears. Fortunately, Tami, Terri, and Mark were all napping.

How sad it was to see so many things go up in smoke—many things our churches had provided. It was especially discouraging to realize that our colored slides of the kids, wedding slides, school yearbooks, and many other things that had special meaning were gone or seriously damaged. When I returned from Aunt Mable's, the fire department was there. I found Mark standing up in his crib seemingly amused with the "pretty" sight he saw out his window. Tami and Terri soon awoke and we explained things to them without getting them too alarmed. We realized God had graciously given each one a calm temperament. It was something I had prayed for many times before they were born.

The day after the fire, we went into Baldwin to get shots for either cholera or typhoid. As we walked into the hospital hand in hand with the twins and carrying Mark, I thanked God silently that we were all alive and well. It truly taught us what was most important in life. Sometimes God has to remind us of those things that matter most. How we thank Him for His nearness in times of trouble and in situations that we don't always understand. He is still with us and will never leave us. "For the things which are seen are temporary but the things which are not seen are eternal" (2 Cor. 4:18).

Summer was already coming to a close as we finished our packing and God graciously replenished many of the things that had been lost. Our barrels and crates were sent to Home of Peace in Oakland, California, a facility that aids missionaries departing to countries in the Far East. Glady had come up from Illinois to help us pack for which I was so thankful. I had been plagued with severe headaches during that time and she helped me so much. She had to take a bus back to Illinois as she and Tom were heading somewhere on vacation. I had to say my goodbyes as she left on the bus. The rest of the family got together at the little cottage and our friends, the Richardsons also came from Greenwood.

The day arrived when we bid tearful goodbyes to our families and headed for the West Coast, stopping to visit our Powell, Wyoming, church where we had served for two summers. In San Francisco we stayed with college friends, Joe and Florence Leach. We were so blessed in renewing our friendship with them. Florence is a nurse and she was so helpful with a miserable allergy problem I had. I am grateful to her to this very day. She introduced me to a medication she was taking which worked perfectly for me and I was able to get it over-the-counter in the Philippines. It is now available everywhere in the U.S. God is often a step ahead of us since He knows our needs. Before we call, He answers and He often uses others in the family of God to accomplish the task and blesses both the giver and receiver.

Kids with Grandma on departure morning

All packed and ready to go

# Chapter 15

## *Trauma on the High Seas*

The day soon came when we boarded *"The Troubadour,"* a Norwegian Freighter heading for the Philippines. I will never forget climbing aboard that ship with our innocent little children, wondering what was in store for us. Soon we were sailing under the Golden Gate Bridge watching the good old U.S.A. slip out of sight. All we could do was look forward to a new land that we hoped would eventually feel like home.

We were shown to our cabins, set up Mark's crib, and began to get organized. We soon discovered that we were five of eight total passengers on the ship. There was an older married couple and a young Jewish actor. We soon became well acquainted while eating together at the captain's table each day.

Our children were an attraction to everyone, which helped us get acquainted with the crew as well. We soon realized the crew was made up of several Filipinos as well as Chinese, Norwegians, and others. Since Steve is a full-blooded Norwegian, he often plied the captain and others with questions and managed to learn a few Tagalog words from the Filipinos aboard.

I have never been a lover of the water and the ocean was a formidable sight to me. However, washing diapers and other items kept me occupied nearly every day. There was no dryer, but a clothesline on the deck served just fine except when it rained of course. One rainy day the older woman passenger slipped on the deck and broke her wrist. She was in great pain and pleaded for someone to get a rescue helicopter to take her to get it set. That wasn't possible, however, so the first-mate did his best to position it and wrap it firmly. We understand that when a doctor finally checked it, he said he couldn't have done better himself.

The weather was quite unpredictable in the tropical seas and eventually we were in the midst of three typhoons crossing each other. Our water glasses would slide from one end of the table to the other. Some folks got seasick. We were okay but didn't have much of an appetite. We also craved some ordinary food. The cooks were great but they did everything in excess and sometimes we would have certain things over and over again due to the lack of new food supplies. The waves were about twenty-five feet high and we would ride up one and down the other, making it difficult to keep our balance when walking on the ship. One night, we had to tie Mark's crib to a doorknob to keep it from sliding across the cabin floor. He, of course, would never remember this, as he was only eight months old. Neither would he remember the celebration on the top deck the night he got his first tooth. The captain decided we should celebrate and have a barbecue. All went fine until the grill tipped over, spilling hot coals on the deck causing it to catch fire momentarily. That was the first traumatic event on our journey.

There was no air-conditioning on the ship so we began to really feel the heat, as we got closer to the Philippines. They had a canvas swimming pool on board so we let the kids enjoy a little splashing around to cool off. However, it proved to be a problem for Tami as she broke out with hives after being in it. I recall having to go up to the top deck at night as she had difficulty getting to sleep. It was a bit cooler up there and I could rock her in a lawn chair. I guess we eventually got some kind of medication to apply to her and eventually the hives went away. That was the second trauma we experienced.

While the typhoons were on, I remember having some fears about the ship staying upright. No one else seemed worried, but one morning I saw Steve up early looking out the portholes and I remember thinking, *I wonder if he's scared and if he's scared, I am really scared.* I knew all I could do was rest in the Lord. One morning Steve went up on the bridge of the ship at sunrise. He saw a sight he had never seen before or since. The sun was shining brightly over the horizon and on each side of the sun were about five more suns reflected, each one getting a little dimmer the farther it was from the sun itself. He has used this as an illustration of Christ the Son being the One we are to emulate and the closer to Him we are the more our lives reflect Him. As we move farther away, our light for Him becomes dim. Certainly there are lessons to learn wherever we are, if we are looking for them.

One day the crewman assigned to steer the ship let Steve try his hand at steering. When he looked back to see the trail behind him, he saw a zigzag pattern and the crewman decided he'd better take over before the captain got concerned. Steve found it was more difficult than it looked. Sometimes life is like that and we need help from above to navigate our earthly pathway. Thank God, He is always there to steer us aright.

Added to the typhoons, we also had engine trouble and had to sit still for about a half a day. The weather was extremely hot that day and the noisy crew working on the engine added to our frustration. "Cabin fever" had set in and we were getting anxious for a place to call home.

Then one particular day the worst trauma hit. Suddenly Terri came to us saying, "I can't find Tami." We could not find Tami anywhere on the ship. The captain, crew, and everyone joined in the search. The last time she had been seen was on the deck and the toys she had been playing with were still there. With panic in our voices, we combed that ship calling out her name. We had checked our cabins and everywhere we knew to look. Our Terri to this day gets knots in her stomach when we retell this story. I must admit I do too. Silently I prayed, *Lord, you know we are going out to serve you, you wouldn't take our daughter would you?"* We looked overboard at the dark swirling water, wondering if she had fallen over the rail and Steve even considered jumping in but decided to check our cabin one more time. Praise God, he found her curled up on a bed behind the door so she wasn't visible when he opened the door. It was strange indeed to find her taking a nap on her own accord and that she was sleeping so soundly she didn't hear her name being called. I have wondered if she was just plain worn out from the rash she had gotten, causing her not to sleep well. At any rate we gave her lots of hugs and praised the Lord together as the crew rejoiced with us.

The captain knew we were going to be missionaries so he asked Steve to lead a service one of the Sundays we were on board the ship. Steve chose to speak on John 10 concerning the Shepherd and the sheep. Steve's family had at one time raised sheep on their farm so he used the illustration of calling the sheep. He was taught by his dad to call them by saying "Kon-Chee-Ta." When the sheep heard the call, they would come running. One day a neighbor boy asked if he could call the sheep. He used the same word, but the sheep didn't even look up. They didn't recognize the voice. Jesus said that is true. In John 10:4 where speaking of the shepherd he said, "And when he brings out his own sheep, he goes before them; and the sheep follow him, for they know his voice." Then Jesus explained in verse 14, "I am the good shepherd; and I know my sheep, and am known by My own." He also adds in verse 27, "My sheep hear my voice, and I know them and they follow Me." There were several applications Steve made in that message but after the message, the captain explained the word he had used to call the sheep was in Norwegian. His dad taught him the word but he never knew its meaning, "Come animals, come and eat." So he had an interesting lesson in Norwegian that day as the crew also learned new truth about our Good Shepherd, the only Shepherd who knows what it's like to be a sheep. Remember how John the Baptist referred to Him? He said, "Behold the Lamb of God who takes away the sin of the world" (John 1:29b).

As we drew near to the Philippines, hints of land became visible and we saw people out in outrigger canoes or fishing boats. Then it was that our Tami crawled up in one of the round portholes in the stateroom, oblivious to her audience and sang her own little song of spontaneous praise to God, "Thank you, God, for letting us see the land. Thank you, God, for letting us see the land." Everyone agreed for it truly was a victory after all the trauma on the sea.

We arrived in Manila after dark and noticed many Filipinos climbing over the side of the ship. The captain warned us about the gangs that hung around the harbor, ready to see what they could steal such as cigarettes or other items from the U.S. Consequently, we were a bit wary of our surroundings when we learned that we were unable to dock that night due to the harbor being full. However, our missionary field chairman, Orman

Knight, and missionary, David Billings, met us on a small launch that we then rode to shore. It was a bit scary as we were still in deep waters with our little ones and cabin belongings. This was an open-air launch that had no protective sides on it as I recall. Remember, I've always had a fear of deep water and the previous incident with Tami didn't help. Steve had other concerns as he was handed a sum of money he was told was more than these Filipinos made in a year so he was told to guard it with his life. Only recently did I learn of the twins' fears of being separated from us as people were hurriedly shoved into several small launches. Fortunately we were kept together.

Thankfully, we made it to shore, and were in Orman's Volkswagen bus going through Manila traffic with constant sounding of the horn. *Where are they taking us?* We wondered. *Where will we sleep tonight?*

# Chapter 16

*Phil-Am Life*

It was September 18, 1965. As we rode through Manila we noticed the streets were wet from the gentle rain, which had preceded us. The humidity hung heavy in the air but the temperature was quite comfortable. I immediately noticed a unique smell—sort of a fruity aroma. To this day that is a memory that surfaces at the mention of the Philippines, as that fragrance is very prevalent throughout the country. We were taken to our first home in the Philippines where we would reside during our time of formal language study.

About 7:00 p.m. we arrived in the Phil-Am Life Compound in Quezon City, the capitol city of Rizal Province. This community was built by the Philippine-American Life Insurance Company and was a very desirable place for us to begin our missionary life. An enclosed, guarded compound, it provided some degree of security. The house was a rather cute little bungalow built mostly of concrete, with a very small kitchen, a living-dining room combination, three bedrooms, a bath and large screened porch at the back of the house. The maids' quarters and their bathroom were just off from the kitchen. A carport was attached to the side of the house with a laundry area outside at the back. A concrete wall surrounded the yard with gates at the carport and front door entrance. Grass covered the entire yard accompanied by a large mango tree, and other shrubs, flowering bushes, and trees.

Immediately after our arrival, missionary Art Beals and Philippine Pastor Fred Magbanua and wife, Aliw, came to welcome us. Fred was the pastor of the Capitol City Baptist Church, just outside of the Phil-Am Life compound and Art Beals was assigned there. What a joy it was to meet these godly people. It was such a contrast from those who swarmed our ship as we arrived. Soon Dave and Ruth Billings, also with our mission, brought our first house girl. Her name was Naty (pronounced Nah'-tee) and though we never got to interview her, she was one of the best we ever had. We were told she couldn't speak English so that put us a bit on edge. We had no idea how to keep her occupied, for as yet we had none of our belongings off the ship. The next day, however, we saw her sweeping the yard with a small broom she found outside. We learned this was a common yard instrument called a walis tingting, a small broom made from the spines of a coconut palm. Its purpose was comparable to our use of a rake. We found her to be very industrious and she actually knew enough English to understand us and was very loving to the children.

The house was temporarily furnished with donations from other missionaries with cots for sleeping, a small rattan couch and a table and chairs. As we prepared for bed that night, Steve killed a huge cockroach and noticed a bullet hole in the back door that gave him concern for our safety. We finally relaxed and had a pretty good night of rest. We were a bit puzzled though the next morning when Steve saw that same cockroach moving across the floor. He said, "I was sure I killed that thing last night." Then he discovered the ants were carrying it away. Cockroaches are huge in the Philippines and later

I found they had chewed many holes in my favorite dress. We were getting acclimated pretty quickly.

Our house in Phil-Am. (Note the Christmas star)

The following day was Sunday and we had more culture shock as we attended Capital City Baptist Church. For us, we saw a sea of black hair and everyone looked alike. That was soon to change as we got to know these people individually. Of course our children got lots of attention with their light skin and hair. Don and Alice Benson, our missionary colleagues, invited us to lunch that day. We ate lechon, which is a roast pig. Filipinos desire the fatty sections most but we knew better than to try that. For dessert we had a very tasty Filipino fruit called lanzones that we came to love. It grows in clusters like grapes with a sort of yellow or tan color skin. The clear colored pulp is in sections like a citrus, though more like a grape in texture. We discovered it has a very large, bitter, seed. If anyone happened to bite into it that awful taste lingered for quite a while. Steve happened to be the "lucky" one to do so and it affected him the entire day.

That afternoon, Dave Billings drove Steve down to the

harbor to see if our ship had docked. We were hoping to get our belongings but it was not yet possible. On the way, Steve got very sick to his stomach and warned Dave about it. Dave's response was "Just hang your head out the window, they'll think you're just another drunk sailor." Since there was no alternative, that's just what he did!

About our third day in the Philippines, the Bensons asked us to go with them to see Taal Volcano in Cavite Province as it had just erupted for the first time in many years. We took the girls but had to leave Mark with Naty. I was very hesitant to leave him but everyone said it would be fine. He seemed to do all right, for which we were very thankful. The volcano eruption was quite spectacular. It changed the appearance of the area, creating a new lake within an island. On the way home we stopped to see another tourist attraction, the bamboo pipe organ in a Catholic Church in the area. It was very unusual indeed. Later we learned that violins, flutes, vibraharps and many other instruments are made of bamboo. We were privileged to hear a children's bamboo orchestra on one occasion.

The first few months were spent trying to get settled and purchase furniture that had to be manufactured there. We learned that things just don't move as fast in the Philippines and there were many trips to downtown Manila and lots of delays. I began to sew curtains and emptied barrels of our belongings. The clothes needed to be put in closets and there were many other tasks. It was interesting to learn about the local brands of food such as butter, cheese, mayonnaise, ketchup etc. and to learn about the various vegetables and fruits that were different from ours. Naty usually purchased our vegetables and fruit at the open market. Later we were able to order fresh produce from Baguio in the mountains. Occasionally we were even able to get strawberries and rhubarb from there. There were certain times when a truck would bring the produce to Manila. It was a treat to make rhubarb pie and strawberry-rhubarb jam.

Tami and Terri turned five while living in Phil-Am and had many playmates, both American and Filipinos, in the area. We had a birthday party for them with many little friends as well as some adults including some of our language teachers who helped us with the games. We still have a tape (now transferred to a CD) interviewing those who were there. The twins began kindergarten at Faith Academy so many of these friends told about the work of their parents in various parts of the Philippines. They had school only four days of the week but it was all day long, due to the fact they had to ride the Faith Academy bus with all the older students. The kindergarten kids brought their lunches each day and had a banig (straw or woven mat) to lie on for a nap in the afternoon. It was a good experience for them but the bus was not air-conditioned and one day as Naty went to meet the bus, she came home carrying Tami who had fainted from the heat. Naty was visibly shaken at this event.

Mark learned many of the twins' school songs and thought he was as big as they were. He had his first birthday in this place and though there was no one his age close by, his sisters and their friends, Paul and Beth Beals and others entertained him very well. He became very adventurous at times and tried to climb on things and desperately wanted to open the front gate. For some reason, he thought life was more interesting across the street. One day, to our dismay, he succeeded and we found him at the neighbor's where he had shed his diaper under a mango tree.

Naty was very good at teaching him to count in Tagalog and sing Tagalog songs. He learned to talk very early and amazed everyone with his vocabulary. However, he seemed to have a problem with his sisters' names. Pointing at Terri, I asked him, "Who's this?" He said, "Dat's Terri." Then pointing at Tami, I said, "Who's that?" He answered, "Dat's anunner Terri." He eventually figured it out. The kids all loved Naty and Mark was especially attached to her since he was alone with her so much when we were in language school. On one occasion when he wasn't too happy about going to bed, he said, "I go sleep with Naty," and headed toward her room.

Mark before his curls were cut off

Steve took several survey trips into outlying areas to see other mission works and to determine where the Lord might be sending us after our language studies. He also got involved working with some Bible school students at the Philippine Missionary Institute (PMI) in Cavite, near the Taal Volcano area. Along with these students, he had several Bible studies in Cavite as well as in the Manila area. These continued as we later began our Tagalog language studies at Interchurch Language School in Quezon City. He often got some unique reactions as he knocked on doors in the provincial area. One day a little girl came to the door and recognizing him as having been there on previous occasions, called out to the family, "Narito and Dios, Narito and Dios" which meant, "God is here, God is here." That stirred an awesome feeling within him, that's for sure. Another time, someone told him, "You smell like God." He couldn't imagine what that meant, for all he wore for fragrance was Right Guard Deodorant. One never knows what reaction you can get from people in another land and culture but we thank God there were several who accepted Christ during that time.

Pastor Ramos, Steve, and Rholly Sabater

We got to know many of our teachers very well and had some of them in our home. Several are still in touch with us via Facebook and other means. How different things are today from the day we first arrived in the Philippines! We didn't have a phone in Phil-Am as this was only our temporary home and it would have taken us over a year or more to get one. This was something that caused us problems from time to time and it was especially so when Steve was away on one of his survey trips.

One day, Terri accidently stepped on my little toe. She was wearing flip flops with a leather sole. It wasn't particularly painful so I forgot about it till later when I noticed I had a red streak going up my leg. I couldn't believe this could come from such a tiny foot on a tiny child but it sure looked like blood poisoning to me. The only medical book I had was Dr. Spock's book for children and it said to get to a doctor immediately if there is a red streak. We had a missionary doctor who lived up the street a ways but unfortunately he was out on a jaunt in one of the provinces. I found there was a Filipino doctor a little further up the street so I went to see him. He told me, "Just keep it dry but if you'd like, you can go to the Phil-Am drug store and get some penicillin pills." It seemed wise, so I followed his directions. The next day the streak was up toward the groin. Fortunately, Steve came home and told me I had better keep my foot in hot water. His college roommate had blood poisoning once and that was the doctor's advice for him. Soon the missionary doctor came home and when informed about the situation, he told me I should have had a penicillin shot right away and that I was fortunate to be alive. We soon realized how quickly infections could get started in that hot humid climate. Again we thank our Heavenly Father for watching over us and meeting every need.

Another time when Steve was gone, Tami got very sick with severe diarrhea and vomiting. I didn't know what to do, as there was no medical doctor nearby. Sonja Beals said I should get her to American Hospital to see Dr. Dill, the American doctor, who was presently in the country. She offered to take care of Terri along with her own four children, but I had to get someone to take care of Mark. Naty was gone to visit her family in a distant province since this was during the holiday season, New Year's Eve to be exact. I had no choice but to leave him with our yard boy's wife whom I had barely met. I gave her instructions on how to heat his baby food and prayed God would care for my baby as we headed off with Tami who was desperately ill. Dr. Dill thought she either had appendicitis or a collapsed intestine. Both were serious and we had to wait until we knew the diagnosis to begin any treatment. I kept praying that God would reveal it soon.

The hospital staff brought me some food that included chocolate cake. Tami saw it and said, "Yum, chocolate cake." And I had to tell her she wasn't allowed to eat it. Then I went into the bathroom and cried my eyes out and prayed. A new thought struck me, *I wonder if it could be food poisoning.* I asked Tami if she had eaten anything that didn't taste good. She mentioned that she ate a bite of some luncheon meat the other night when we were gone to a meeting and it didn't taste good so she didn't eat any more of it. I asked Dr. Dill if one bite could cause food poisoning. He said, "It sure could." Eventually he gave her some soda crackers and she kept them down. He decided that it must be food poisoning. They watched her carefully through the night and we tried to sleep. Firecrackers were going off at the church across the street and elsewhere throughout the city. That is what goes on in the Philippines on New Years' Eve. It felt more like the Fourth of July to us but we certainly were not celebrating!

We were thankful to get home the next morning, only to find out that the woman taking care of Mark had boiled water, dumped the contents of the baby food jar into the water and tried to feed it to Mark. I don't know if he burned his mouth or what but I don't think he ate much. How good it was to be back together as a family safe and sound. "Daddy" had returned and there were hugs for everyone. Now we could celebrate.

The twins were flower girls in several weddings

Our kids with Beth and Paul Beals

# Chapter 17

*Trials and Triumphs*

Language study and Bible studies, as well as other ministries, kept us busy. If we had any doubt that music could be used of the Lord on the mission field, it was soon forgotten. We found it to be a great avenue of ministry, especially in the Philippines. Filipinos love music and many are very talented in playing instruments and often have beautiful singing voices. We had many opportunities to sing in provincial churches as well as in greater Manila. We often sang at "Christ for Greater Manila," an evangelistic effort in downtown Manila. We also took part in a Christmas "Messiah" concert which involved several churches in the area. A Christian medical doctor, who was a great musician, directed this.

FEBIAS (Far Eastern Bible Institute and Seminary) invited us to teach some summer courses as long as we were in Manila. I taught music theory and Steve taught the Bible classes. We sang at Christmas programs and a graduation ceremony. Ruth Robinson, a FEBIAS graduate, who later attended our Philippine Bible study here in East Phoenix, remembered us from "Christ for Greater Manila" meetings. We did not know her while in the Philippines but she told me I sang at her graduation from FEBIAS. Ruth and her husband Nate now head up Children's Concern in the Philippines that feeds and ministers to homeless children. They have also taken over our Philippine Bible study in the east valley of Phoenix.

Far East Broadcasting Company is near FEBIAS and has programs in many languages throughout Asia. We were privileged to record about a dozen solos and duets for their radio station, DZAS. We came across the audiotape nine years ago when looking for our wedding tape, hoping to play it at our Golden Wedding Anniversary. We never found the wedding tape as many tapes had been ruined due to the heat and humidity of the Philippines and the hot and dry weather of Arizona. We did, however, discover the DZAS tape where most of our songs were still audible. A man in our church was able to copy it to a C.D. Having been recorded in 1966, the songs are old so our son, Mark, who is an artist, used a vintage style motif and titled it, "Songs of Yesteryear." It was given to guests at our anniversary celebration. Those old songs still ministered to many, especially to those within our age group.

Language school was difficult but we learned much in our classes and integration sessions that involved speaking only Tagalog in a social setting. After one of these sessions we were always glad to be at home in our own house where we could relax and speak our own language again. Attending the language school gave us a greater knowledge of Philippine culture as well. Often we would have social gatherings where native songs and dances would be a part of the festivities. We learned to sing some Tagalog folk songs and were asked to wear native clothing and sing some classic Filipino songs at one of the language school parties. We had friends among our classmates, some of whom became life-long friends. They were affiliated with various denominations and missions, which also broadened our learning experience.

Singing at Language School party

We found, however, that we did not always have time for everything we wanted or needed to do because of our studies. Mark would often need attention when we needed to study. Babies always seem to need their mommy and I found I could not spend as much time on studies because my children were always my first priority. God was gracious and helped me to learn the language sufficiently to get by and to continue my studies little by little.

We had to make trips to downtown Manila in order to get our mail so we of course could not go every day. Sometimes our fellow missionaries would get our mail when they went down since we all had the same post office box. However, one day after we hadn't gotten any mail for a long time, we decided we'd better go down and do our duty. I recall getting a box from a church somewhere back home with various goodies. Among them was a small braided rug. I'm sure it was sent with good intentions but we could not get that rug to lie flat on the floor. It continued to curl up no matter what we would do to flatten it. We all laughed about it and decided it would be a good bed for our dog.

We didn't know how quickly laughter could turn to tears, as the next envelope we opened was from a "recording company." Inside we found a cablegram from Hildi, simply stating, "Glady and Tom killed in car accident." Funeral date and place was shown. We could not believe our eyes. We had just gotten a letter from them not long before saying they were even thinking of joining us in the Philippines when Tom finished his Ph.D. studies. We noticed the funeral date was already past. We had no phone to call home, no way to send flowers or express our sympathies. I can't recall what we did as far as making contact. We must have gone to our fellow-missionary's home to use their phone. All I can remember was my first reaction, though I didn't say it aloud, *Why, God, why?* I recalled several dreams I had while still in the states. In one of the dreams Glady had been killed and Tom was beside himself with grief. Another time I dreamed Tom and been killed and Glady was grief stricken. Recalling the dreams, I began to wonder if God was trying to prepare me for this very time. A measure of peace came into my mind: *They are together.*

Tom and Glady

However, it did not ease the pain of losing the sister I used to play with as my doll, placing her in my doll buggy and adoring her all those years, enjoying her cute and humorous ways. I remembered taking her to kindergarten her first day of school. I sewed clothes for her. Her letters during my college days usually included some original cartoons or other illustrations of her latest hairstyle or dress she was sewing. They were killed in a head-on collision in the Chicago area. The other driver, also killed in the accident, was a born-again Christian as well. God must have wanted all of them home.

Tami and Terri arrived home from kindergarten that day and seeing my tears, knew something was wrong. We explained what had happened and I remember so well Tami's response, "Well, Mommy, you shouldn't cry because Aunt Glady and Uncle Tom are up in heaven with Jesus." I thank God for the faith that was instilled in them at an early age. Often a little child shall lead us with such simplicity of faith. I didn't know how we could face the days ahead; however, we knew God must have a plan. We could not understand all of this although in time we would.

Glady had several miscarriages during her short married life and it was discovered that she too had a divided uterus just as Hildi did. Both my paternal and maternal grandparents married first cousins, which was quite common in their day, and we have wondered if that was what caused this strange defect. I realized how blessed I was not to have had the problem that plagued both of my sisters. I don't deserve God's goodness but how I praise Him for it. I also realize "For everyone to whom much has been given, from him much will be required; and to whom much has been committed, of him they will ask the more" (Luke 12:48b).

Within the next week a missionary with the Navigator's mission, who lived across the street from us, lost her husband in a motorcycle accident. I was able to spend some time with her and encourage her by sharing my grief with her.

When we left for the Philippines, my dad was very upset that we were leaving him to go so far away. He did write letters though and it wasn't long until we got a letter we will never forget. He said He had asked Jesus to take away his drinking and smoking as he had come to the place where he knew he could not do it himself. He said God just took the desire completely away. He now could not stand the smell of alcohol or cigarettes. He made some remark about Glady and Tom's death playing a part in this. He was witnessing to his friends and was so happy to know he was right with God. As I looked back, I recall many tests God put Dad through; yet it seems until God took his pride and joy, the youngest child, who was as gregarious as he, he wasn't about to make that break. His hardened heart had now become tender enough to let the Savior in and God was gracious to help him through his addiction with no withdrawal problems because he thrust himself helplessly on Christ. Self must be put to death as we lean entirely on Him in surrender. As long as we think we can do anything ourselves, it will not work.

As difficult as it was to lose Glady and Tom, we are so thankful for the change in a dad that we had prayed for since we were small children. There is always something to praise God for and once again we saw the value and privilege of prayer, not the prayer itself, but the fact that it was directed to the all-powerful One who loves, forgives, and shows abundant mercy. God has promised to listen and answer prayer and He never breaks His promise.

Glady and Tom's death occurred on September 7, 1966, after we had just been in the Philippines for a year. Now we were getting close to our second Christmas abroad and missing our extended families that were always there for us. Added to this was the great loss and grief over losing Glady and Tom. We knew this would be a difficult Christmas for my family especially. We remembered with thankful hearts, that Christmas a few years back when the whole family got snowed in and we had them all under our roof. God gave us that special time and we'll never have another like it until we are together in our heavenly home.

# Chapter 18

## *Visitors from Home*

God did something very special for us at a time when we needed it most, and put it in the hearts of Steve's sisters, Charlotte and Phoebe, yet unmarried, to come and spend several weeks over Christmas with us. It gave us something to look forward to and it certainly broadened their knowledge of our work and ministry. They were quite an attraction to people wherever they went. People wanted to touch Charlotte's blonde hair and would often run from the back of a shop to see her. Both girls were very attractive and at their prime of life at the time.

We chose to spend our Christmas vacation in Baguio, the only cool place in the Philippines. We also traveled further north to see the Banawe rice terraces and visit Bontoc where the Ifugao tribal people live. We will never forget the drive up the mountains on those formidable roads. With one lane only, it was impossible to pass another vehicle, and we met several trucks and busses. Added to that, the road was wet and muddy from heavy rains at that time. The edge of the road dropped a long way down to who knows where. Somehow we made it but often had to back up to a better spot to allow passage of another vehicle. In Bontoc we visited the Habich family who worked among the Ifugaos. Gundy Habich was a tall basketball player at Northwestern College when we were there as students, and his children attended Faith Academy.

Their daughter, Dana, was a classmate to the twins but about twice their size in height. They didn't meet till years later when Dana was a boarding student at Faith Academy. This was a great reunion for us as adults and a thrilling experience for Charlotte and Phoebe. It was a bit frightening, however, to learn that someone recently had taken the life of another by spearing him in the back while he walked in front of the Habich's home.

With the Habich family in Banawe

The Ifugao people, formerly known for headhunting, are different in appearance from the lowland Filipino. They have a more rugged build and the men wear G-strings and an occasional jacket if it is cold, but always they are barefoot even in town in Baguio. The women likewise are barefoot, wear hand-woven tribal wrap-around skirts, snake bones in their hair and some type of simple shirt. That area is changing though as Banawe now has a modern hotel and hospital. Though there was a recent beheading, these things were also beginning to change due to the influence of missionaries. Truly God's Word gives light and it was evident in several ways.

We visited a small shop in Bontoc where the woman proprietor had arms covered with tattoos and snake bones around her head. In Tagalog, we asked her about the price of a certain item to which she answered in perfect English, "I'm sorry, I don't speak Tagalog." We then learned she had children studying at a large university in Manila and was pretty up to date with modern life.

We spent the remainder of our time in Baguio, the vacation place for most missionaries. It is a mile-high city about two hundred miles north of Manila. Our mission rented a vacation house and each family chose a block of time set aside for its vacation. It was far from fancy but it was a place for us to stay and we could drive to carving villages, the markets around the area, and just enjoy the fireplace at night.

Our housegirls, Naty and Vising

John Hay, fomerly a U.S. Air Base in Baguio, was a recreation place for the military to relax and recuperate. There was a lovely golf course with a clubhouse called the Nineteenth Tee. We enjoyed going out there for stateside ice cream or a hamburger and often would meet other missionaries there. Though not a golfer, Steve tried golfing one day and met President Marcos on the green. He greeted him properly and the president was very cordial in return.

Annual conferences for our mission were occasionally held in Baguio if sufficient housing was available for all of us. We have many fond memories of that place in the mountains. We visited the woodcarving villages and the school where silver is spun into thin strands to make lovely jewelry. There was also a weaving school where native fabrics are woven and made into various items of clothing as well as table linens. Baguio provided many interesting adventures as well as a means of purchasing gifts for those who supported us in our work.

Soon our vacation time was over and we had to head back to Manila and our language studies. Before leaving Baguio, Charlotte and Phoebe each purchased a ring from the Chinese proprietor of a Chinese gift shop. Phoebe's was a pearl ring and Charlotte's, a jade. The gold was mined there in Baguio and the genuine pearls were from the Mindanao deep sea. The woman's husband created the lovely gold settings. This Chinese woman was an interesting person whom we would come to know better in subsequent visits to Baguio.

On our way home to Manila, we couldn't help but notice the beautiful Christmas star lanterns on most of the homes along the way. This is perhaps the primary decoration for the Filipino homes at Christmas time. Like the rest, our home looked cheerful with its red and white star lantern at the front door as though welcoming us home.

It was soon time for Charlotte and Phoebe to leave. It was also time for us to get back to the daily routine of language-learning and our eventual move to the provincial area for the remainder of our term. Life would be different in the province but God was with us and we continued to look to Him as we prepared for this change in our lives.

Through much prayer and advice from others of our senior missionaries, we learned that our new assignment would be in Quezon Province about one hundred miles south of Manila in Lucena City where Rogelio (Roger) and Flor Baldemor had started a church along with Leonard and Jeanette Tuggy. Jake and Gladys Toews had also been involved in the work there. We had worked with Roger's brother Oscar in Cavite in the greater Manila area and knew of Roger through the film, "Heart of the Philippines," the story of his life during stressful times in the Philippines as he searched for the truth. Roger was a dynamic preacher and his wife was a FEBIAS graduate in Christian education. They had just seen a new church building built in Lucena so it was with eagerness that we began to pack up and get ready for the next adventure in our lives. We had secured a home to rent there and were at peace with God's leading in our lives.

The mission had secured a huge truck for the move to Lucena. We thought we were doing pretty well with our packing until the truck arrived a day early. From the unpleasant odor we knew it had been used in the fishing industry. Nevertheless, we hurriedly started loading and headed south to our new provincial home.

# Chapter 19

*Provincial Life*

Lucena, a city of about 100,000 in population is surrounded by mountains, ocean beaches, coconut trees, and fishing villages. The scenery is lovely with a climate similar to Manila.

Our home was very nice as far as provincial housing goes. It was built of predominantly concrete and we loved the layout. There was a large carport that led into the lowest level where we had our office, schoolroom, and a bathroom. Because this was a separate level of the house, the office was very convenient for housing the many guests we had. Up a few more steps was a large sala (living room) that was on a level by itself. It had a pond and rock garden that ran into one side of the room from the outdoor fishpond by the front door entrance. Up a few more steps from the sala, was the dining room and kitchen with a hallway leading to the bedrooms, from which it was possible to look down into the sala. The laundry area was outside below the kitchen and clotheslines were under the carport, a good feature, since we didn't have a dryer and frequently had rainy weather.

Our home in Lucena City (Quezon Province)

We arrived in Lucena at 10:00 p.m. June 28, 1967. We were informed that the Lucena Baptist Church and the neighboring town of Sariaya were in the midst of an evangelistic crusade. Sariaya was known as the "Little Rome of Quezon Province" because it was predominately Roman Catholic. A large part of our ministry was focused on trying to get a church started in Sariaya, which we were able to do before we left for furlough. We also worked with Pastor Rogelio and Mrs. Flor Baldemor in the Lucena church seeking to see it further built up by encouraging and training the believers.

Mark now four years old, was waiting for me to get ready for church. He looked up at me and said, "Mommy, Eric Kurtz (another missionary kid) says Jesus isn't up in heaven. He is in our hearts." I told him that was true only if we asked Him to come into our hearts and asked him to take our sins away. He immediately, without prompting, stood and bowed his head, asking Jesus to come into his heart. I was so blessed by his immediate obedience. Later as he got older, he reinforced that decision when he understood more of the implications of what it meant to give his life to Christ and live for Him.

My work was predominantly with the youth of the Lucena Church and training a choir. One year Flor Baldemor translated into Tagalog the Christmas program I had written for the Dallas Christian Grade School and the next year we were able to have a choir present one of John Peterson's cantatas, "A Song Unending." We invited one of our own missionaries, Joy Limburg, a Faith Academy teacher, to accompany us. We also had a soloist from Manila along with several gifted soloists from Lucena. They were so thrilled to learn to sing in parts as they followed the notation. The men, particularly, couldn't believe they actually had learned to sing tenor or bass.

We had a nice dinner in our home after the cantata where we brought in square bamboo tables and chairs to fill up our sala. Each table had a Christmas centerpiece. A neighbor who loved to sing the Philippine kundimans (Classic Philippine folk songs similar to opera) came to entertain us. It was a night they will always remember. Some of the choir wanted to learn more music so I was able to have a few workshops teaching them some basic music theory. I used Tagalog as much as I was able but with some of the musical terms I had to resort to English. Almost all Filipinos know some English, as it is a standard requirement in their school curriculum. It is mostly the older people who have difficulty with English.

One of the young men from our previous work in Cavite province, Rholando Sabater, a graduate of Philippine Missionary Institute, came with us to Lucena. We called him Rholly (Roh-lee). He hadn't finished high school so we helped him finish there in Lucena. He had a room at the church but ate his evening meal at our house every day. Rholly was a very handsome young man and had a very gregarious personality so he easily made friends and influenced those around him. One day he befriended an American Peace Corp worker, Don Good, from the neighboring town of Tayabas. He brought him to our home to introduce him to us. Steve soon came to know Don and took him skin diving to get better acquainted. Don heard Steve's testimony and soon accepted the Lord. He came to church and sang in our choir and was often in our home. Later, Don went back to the States, attended seminary, married and returned with CBFMS as a missionary to that very area. Presently He and his wife, Ruth, have decided to retire in the Philippines and continue to serve the Lord as long as they are able. Four decades have passed and we still keep in touch.

A group of young people with Rholly (on the right)

Don Good

After much prayer, I felt led of the Lord to teach Tami and Terri at home. Of all our missionaries, we were the farthest from Faith Academy. The girls were still very small for their age and since I had taught school in the states, I knew I could teach them. This was met with some opposition from our older missionaries but I have never doubted that this was God's will. They did very well and this also allowed them to learn the language and culture. They learned to speak Tagalog with a very good accent so much so that if someone called on the phone and one of them answered, people would ask, "Who was that little Filipino that answered the phone?" One night I heard one of the twins talking in her sleep, using entirely Tagalog. On days when language study was difficult for Steve and me, we facetiously considered going outside to play wondering if we could learn as easily as our kids learned it from their friends.

Potente family

They had some wonderful playmates in the neighborhood including the Potente children whose parents were members of the church. This family lived a block down the street from us. Mr. Joe Potente was a banker and his wife, Emma, was a nurse. Emma had grown up in Iloilo as the daughter of a pastor. Both spoke fluent English and had lovely singing voices. They were a valuable part of our choir and also favored us with solos and duets.

On one occasion I had to take a bus to Manila, which was a new experience for me, so I asked Emma to accompany me. It was a memorable day as it was the day President Nixon was elected and young newsboys called out, "Extra, Extra," as they held up the blazing headline, "Richard Nixon elected president of the United States." Another memory from that day was the trip home to Lucena with pigs and chickens riding along on top of the bus. I also saw a lady get on the bus carrying a small beaded purse in which the beads formed letters that read, "God Knows." At first it puzzled me until I remembered that pickpockets were very prevalent in public places in the Philippines. Apparently she was sending a gentle warning.

Gay, the youngest Potente girl used to come every day to our school room and along with Mark, would join in our music, Bible, and Art classes. Then the two of them would go out and play while I taught the reading, math, and social studies. This provided a good companion for Mark while I was occupied with teaching and Gay enjoyed coming and learned a bit as well.

Our schoolroom with Mark and Gay
Potente in the background

Mark seemed to like to wander. What is it with little boys? Several times he tried to go down to the Potentes, just a block from home. Of course he didn't tell us where he was going. Apparently no one heard him at the gate so he climbed over their wall and then found they weren't home. We found him entertaining himself by the door and he wasn't crying. He was about three years old at this time. Another day we had a lot of company. Other missionaries were at our house and somehow he slipped away without our knowing it. Soon a woman came bringing him home saying she found him on the bridge.

When I heard that, I couldn't believe he would go that far and the scariest part was that bridge had holes in it large enough for him to fall into the river. God obviously watched over him.

The kids would often play downstairs in the laundry area while I was doing the laundry. One day the floor was wet and Tami was rushing around and fell flat on her face on the concrete. She was out cold. I didn't know what to do, so I called Emma, the nurse. I carried Tami up to my room where she came to but said to me, "Mommie, can you turn on the light, I can't see you?" It scared me so much as it was broad daylight. Emma said she might have had a concussion. Eventually she could see but she soon had to throw up and we took her to a local doctor who said she did have a slight concussion. We got instructions on how to care for her and she seemed no worse for the wear the next day. How grateful we are to our Lord who is our very present help in times of trouble.

Another problem we ran into was having a wonderful house girl come down with tuberculosis. Crippled from polio, Juling (pronounced Huling) was a very industrious worker whom the kids loved. They would play hide and seek with her and have the best time. However, we had no choice but to let her go and that meant we had no house help until we could find someone else. It also meant we had to be tested to see if our kids had gotten TB. They had the test in Manila and the provincial doctor read the results. She said Tami and Mark both had it so they had to have shots and some terrible tasting liquid medicine. Eventually, we took them to Manila to St. Luke's Hospital for a check-up. The doctor there asked me to tell him what their skin test looked like. After my description he said his tests showed no evidence that they had TB. He also directed us to stop the medicine or their immunity would be compromised against the disease. I remember that day so well. Some of our fellow-missionaries were at the same hospital and waved at us from a distance down a hallway but would not come near us for fear of infection. All of course were relieved when they found we didn't have the dreaded disease.

The 3 sets of twins in the Lucena Church

Our kids with their puppies

# Chapter 20

## Typhoons, Parasites, and Jellyfish

Other problems plagued us in Lucena. We often had to eat in the homes of our parishioners, especially on Fiesta days such as Christmas Day. Later, we decided to take our vacation in Baguio at that time to avoid this problem. We knew our church people would be hurt if we didn't eat with them and visit in their homes but often we'd be up all night with diarrhea and vomiting. We had one dysentery after another for which we had to be tested in the American Hospital lab in Manila to determine what species it was, and then receive the medications that applied to that particular type. I never will forget when Terri passed a huge tapeworm. It didn't seem to bother her much but when we saw it, it was frightening. How thankful we were she got rid of it. Usually food that was prepared ahead of time and left to sit unrefrigerated or contaminated by flies, was the culprit for bacillic dysentery whereas amoebic dysentery came from impure water. We boiled our own water and tried very hard not to drink anything but soda pop outside of our home.

Lucena had several beaches, one of which was Dalahican. We often visited people there who were fishermen. Most of the fishing was done at night using a dugout canoe with a lantern of some type to attract the fish into a net. It was interesting to learn the different types of fish and the fishing methods. On one occasion, we were visiting a family from the church that lived on a small island in that area. A jellyfish attacked Tami. What a strange sight it was as this clear see-through blob of jelly wrapped itself around her leg. She screamed out in pain. One of the men with us knew what to do, as he was familiar with all of these strange creatures. Discretely, he found a container in which to urinate and poured it on the jellyfish and she was free. Thank the Lord; He knows how to take care of us in every situation. There were also many fish that we enjoyed eating, mostly salt-water fish from the ocean.

Speaking of eating, we missed some of the foods we enjoyed back home, like pumpkin pie. For one of our Thanksgiving dinners I was able to get a squash that tasted just like pumpkin. We were so excited to have pumpkin pie again. Mark thought this was great even though he was too young to have had pumpkin pie in the states. He proudly showed a frequent guest what it looked like all mixed up ready to be poured into the pie shell. Being small, as he was, he pulled the bowl over to him and spilled most all of the contents onto the kitchen floor. We sadly scooped up most of it and baked it anyway and it never did us any harm. We appreciated that pie more than ever after all it had been through!

Strangely, there are also many things we miss now that we are back in the states such as the poinsettias that grew very tall by our front entrance. They enabled us to have a beautiful centerpiece at Christmas time.

We always made it a point to visit the Chinese gift shop while in Baguio. On several occasions, the owner invited us to her apartment behind the shop for tea and cake. We had a little problem eating with chopsticks but managed. She was originally from Shanghai, China, and used to play the piano in a Baptist Church there and had also been a dean of women in a school in China. She related to us that China was such a wonderful place prior to communism and had many valuable artifacts such as ivory and jade tapestries and other lovely things from old China. One day she showed us a huge gold piece worth a great deal, I'm sure. We found out, however, that she left the Baptist Church because her son had been killed and she believed the "gods" were punishing her for leaving her former Buddhist religion. We tried to share truth with her each time we were in Baguio. God would give us continued opportunities to minister to this woman in the future. I began to pray for her regularly and I specifically requested that I might be able to find a book about China prior to communism with a Christian emphasis.

There was a Chinese hotel in Baguio and I recall going with Bill and Flossie Simons, and other missionaries to have dinner there. The Simons were the first missionaries with Conservative Baptists to go to the Philippines. They came because they were put out of China when communism came. I could see how thrilled they were to be with these Chinese people again as we all gathered in an upstairs room for a meal together. It was easy to imagine what it would feel like to be in China. There are many Chinese in the Philippines and they are often referred to as "The Jews of the Orient" as they are very prosperous in their businesses and are found to be hard working and very disciplined. It was a joy to meet some who had become Christians and see how determined they were to be testimonies for the Lord.

Whenever we had to leave our home, we would never leave it unattended. Usually we found a young boy in Lucena or Sariaya who would stay there and watch over things. On one of these occasions, Steve asked Rudy

Bernardo from Sariaya to stay in our house. When we got back he told us someone had come up the back stairs from the laundry area trying to sneak in. Rudy yelled something real loud and the person got so scared he tumbled all the way down the stairs to the cement below. I think that was the only time we had an attempted break in.

While we were in Lucena, we noticed an article in the Manila Times regarding the death of our former neighbor boy in Phil-Am due to a fraternity-hazing incident. He was the brother of three girls Tami and Terri played with almost every day. We were shocked at this terrible event and knew we had to visit this family as soon as we could. When we arrived there, they said, "We knew you would come." How thankful we were that we didn't disappoint them. We shared with them the love of Jesus and His plan for salvation and though they were very interested they made no decision at that time. However, we prayed with them and continued to pray that God's Word would not return void, as He has promised.

We had many beggars come to our gate. I think we even had one person with leprosy. We tried to determine what the real need was and give rather than loan money which worked out well for the most part. There were always some needs you couldn't ignore such as the need for medicine. Many times our carryall became a hearse or an ambulance as the need for it arose.

Typhoons came often everywhere we lived in the Philippines. Earthquakes were also plentiful. A 7.3 magnitude earthquake occurred in 1968 with an epicenter in Manila. It woke us from a sound sleep ninety miles away in Lucena. Steve felt the bed shaking so intensely he nearly fell on the floor. I, on the other hand, was more aware of the handles on our dresser drawers jangling. We experienced earthquakes wherever we lived. This was the earthquake that took down a large apartment building called "Ruby Towers" in Manila.

Our Lucena house had a huge round window made of concrete in sort of a lattice design. It had screen behind it but no glass. I will never forget how we had to move our furniture around to keep it from getting wet when the rain came from that direction. This was especially true during a typhoon as the wind moves in a cyclical motion which necessitated moving the furniture as the wind changed. I recall one day walking across the kitchen to close a window and getting so wet that I had to change clothes.

Storms like this would often cause us to lose our electricity and often our water supply was insufficient to flush toilets or take showers for a few days. On one of those times a Christian basketball team came from the U.S. with the purpose of having an evangelistic outreach. They played a game in Sariaya where they gave testimonies at half-time. I didn't have ice to cool down the boiled water we had to serve them. These are common problems in the tropics but God always supplied somehow in these times of emergency. We don't know what we would do without the Lord who is still our daily guide and provision. He provided our strength from within and shielded us from dangers around us so many times.

We thoroughly enjoyed our time in the provincial area and became very attached to the people. A church was started in Sariaya and Lucena kept growing as well. Many souls came into the kingdom of God and were baptized. Several of our young people from that area have become pastors, teachers, and even missionaries elsewhere. In our old age, we still correspond with them by e-mail and Facebook. To God be the glory!

# Chapter 21

_Provincial Ministry_

## By Steve Sonmor

Lucena and Sariaya were in the midst of an evangelistic campaign when we arrived at our new provincial home. During the day we attempted to get settled in our house and each night we would bring many to Lucena from Sariaya in hired jeepneys. At the end of the campaign one of the men from Sariaya asked me if we would help them get a Conservative Baptist Church started in Sariaya. What an exciting challenge, especially with my very limited facility in Tagalog. Therefore, I spent my mornings studying Tagalog in my office and at various times with my tutor, Mrs. Baldemor, the pastor's wife. In the afternoons and evenings I drove to Sariaya to follow up on the contacts made during the campaign. Pastor Baldemor accompanied me much of the time, which not only gave me a companion who was a virtual expert in the Tagalog language but was an unbelievably good evangelist. I was so blessed to have been able to work with him and he taught me much.

One of the first contacts we dealt with was a husband and wife who made a noodle like substance called "miki" (pronounced meekee), which they would put in little cellophane packages that he would sell to the school kids for a merienda treat during the morning school break. At that time they were charging five centavos per package, which was less than a penny in U.S. currency. Needless to say they were far from being rich. In fact they were so poor they didn't have a single stick of furniture in their house other than that which was made from salvaged 2x4's, tin cans, and split bamboo strips tacked onto some upright 2x4's and bamboo. It was fun to see some of our 4x8x3/4 inch plywood crating from shipping our goods to the Philippines turned into a lovely, large table and benches.

This man was the first of his family to make a decision to receive Jesus as his Savior. There was a marked change, which was obvious to all who knew him. However, his wife was not very happy with his decision. I remember coming to their place one afternoon and I greeted her with "Magandang Hapon, Po" (Good afternoon, Mam). She took one glaring look at me and walked briskly away telling me by her body language that she wasn't especially happy with the change in her husband and pretty much telling me she wanted nothing to do with it. Praise God it wasn't long before she too came under conviction and received Christ as her Savior. This was one of the first families to come out boldly for Christ.

Fortunately, we had one very solid Christian family who was from the church in Lucena originally but this part of the clan was settled in Sariaya and made their living by selling fresh fish in the markets of the various towns in the area. They were a solid Christian family and gave the solidity needed in starting a new work, especially in a town like Sariaya, which was considered one of the foremost Roman Catholic towns in that region of Quezon Province. The head of the family had one set of children by his first wife and when she died he married again and started over with what we saw as his second family. He was very dedicated to the Lord and it was a thrill to me to hear him pray powerfully in the Tagalog language.

Since we were starting a church, a prayer meeting was very important. I figured I'd better try to prepare devotionals in Tagalog for these meetings. Here I was this raw missionary attempting to lead a group of fairly mature Christians to worship in a language which was new to me. I'm sure it sounded like I was attempting to lecture kindergarteners considering how basic was my grasp of the language. In my mind, I can still hear this man pray for my progress in the language. Translated it was, "Oh Lord, the Greatest of All, bless Mr. Sonmor in his study of Tagalog. You know the difficult time he is having."

I would listen to this and go home feeling lower than a snake's belly in my discouragement. He wasn't trying to discourage me, in fact I believe his prayer was intended to give me encouragement but my personality interpreted it as having a very negative connotation. When I look back on it now, I marvel that they had the patience to put up with such a neophyte. They were great people and greatly used of God in seeing the church established in Sariaya.

About two houses away from our first contact was another dear family. The husband was very skilled at mechanics and building windmills. In fact he and his helpers built one windmill that reached above the coconut grove in which it was located so that the fan would be able to catch a good breeze and pump them a ready supply of water. I remember one Saturday night in particular when I came by their place and they invited me in. We had a wonderful time going over the plan of salvation that resulted in both he and his wife praying to receive the Savior before I returned home to Lucena. This family became a very solid part of the church and a great encouragement to a very inexperienced missionary. The proof of their decisions was revealed when they showed up in the morning service in the Lucena Church, as it was quite some time before we could find a place to meet and begin services in Sariaya. He related to Pastor Baldemor his experience from the night before saying, "The way is fairly clear but there are still small willow-like trees blocking my understanding." By the time we began holding services in Sariaya they had become very solid followers of Jesus.

I always enjoyed walking through Philippine markets as there is always something to learn about the people as well as finding something interesting to purchase to bring home as a display of life in the Philippines. One afternoon as I moseyed along through the Sariaya market, I happened to come to a stall where a young woman was selling something. She was very open to listen to my presentation of the gospel and this opened the door to get acquainted with the whole family. They were willing to listen to the gospel but reticent to receive the Savior at that time.

One day the woman I originally contacted in the market came to our home in Lucena. It was obvious that she was very bothered about something. I sought to lead her to the Savior but there was something she was hesitant to reveal to me that was keeping her from that decision. Finally it came out that she was involved in lesbianism. Needless to say, I was shocked as there was nothing obvious about her that would have revealed such a thing. We tried to reach out to her and her lesbian friends but I'm afraid we didn't see the kind of decisions they needed to make.

Life in the tropics is very exhausting and we learned that having a siesta was not a lazy man's thing but was very necessary if you expected to survive in such heat. Not only were siestas necessary, so also were vacation periods. After a week or two in the mountains of Baguio, one could come back to the work refreshed and ready to go at it.

On one of our Baguio vacations we came back to Lucena to a great disappointment. Our contact from the Sariaya market had an emergency in the family with her mom. This lady had listened to the gospel several times but was reticent to make the eternal decision. While we were in Baguio, the mother had a serious heart attack and ended up in the hospital in Lucena. They came looking for me and finally found the Baldemors who told them we were out of town on vacation. They wanted me to talk one more time with the mother but she slipped into eternity before we got home. If only someone had contacted us in Baguio, but no one did. Had they, I'd have driven home to Lucena immediately.

There was another lady we made contact with whose house was at the lower part of Sariaya toward the ocean. Late one afternoon, two of the young people from Sariaya went with me to her house to have a Bible study. As we were progressing with the study I noticed a young lady kind of patrolling the neighborhood as if to keep anyone out who was not Roman Catholic. I invited her to join us in the study, which she did. We then started all over again and I said in Tagalog, "All men are sinners." To which our latest arrival said, "That's true except one person, she has never sinned." I said, "Who is that?" to which she replied, "The Virgin Mary has never sinned." Normally, I would wait to share Luke 1:47 with a Roman Catholic until further into the witnessing process but I felt the Holy Spirit telling me to share this with her right then and there. So I asked her, "What is the condition of a person who needs a Savior?" She then answered, "They are sinners." Then we opened the Bible to Luke 1:46-47 which says, "And Mary said: "My soul magnified the Lord and my spirit has rejoiced in God my Savior." Then I explained to this dear young lady that Mary had declared here in the Bible that she needed a Savior because she was a sinner. Rarely have I seen the power of God's Word make an impact on a person as it did on this girl that afternoon. We then found out she was studying to become a nun in the Catholic Church but God had spoken to her heart and after another year of careful teaching in the Scriptures from the pastor and the people in the Sariaya Church, she came to know Christ as her Savior. As a result of this chance acquaintance we were able to spend time getting to know her parents as well as her immediate and extended family. It also opened the doors to get to know several others in that neighborhood.

At the other side of the town was a lady who had known nothing but bad luck, if luck plays any part in one's life. We still had some of our plywood left from our crating and it was getting near furlough time so we took four long 4x4's and some of the men from the church erected her a small house from these materials. Oh, we didn't see immediate results but I was assured by the believers in the church that the good will that this created in the whole city would pay great dividends some day in the Lord's work in Sariaya.

With about a half year left of our first term we saw services started in the Sariaya Conservative Baptist Church. That was a thrill. The family that lived in front of the home where we held our main Bible studies was willing to rent their house for us to use in the beginning days of the church. I made tables and benches for the kids for Sunday school upstairs and benches for the chapel below in the sala (living room.) We were right on the national highway so we were very visible to all who passed by. It was hard to find grape juice for communion services but a good bottle of sarsi (sarsaparilla, a local soft drink) made a good substitute.

It was surprising how many began attending the services and it was hard for us to leave such a wonderful bunch of God's people to take our furlough in the States. The leadership, in whose hands we left the work, were trustworthy men and women who loved the Lord deeply.

However, our work included a funeral before furlough arrived. It was a Sunday afternoon and I was asked to come to Sariaya to help out this one young mother who was very sick. They came carrying this woman in their arms, as she was so sick. I carried her in my carryall to the hospital in Lucena. No one told me how sick she really was, nor did I have any apprehension she would die that night from cancer, which was far more advanced than anyone let on. So trying to be the good missionary, I went to the local provincial prison and asked the officials to give me prisoners to take to the hospital to give blood for this lady. We filled our Chevy Carryall with prisoners and guards and off we went to get their blood, for which I had to pay them. In the process of doing all this hauling some guy drove his tricycle (motorcycle with a sidecar) right behind my vehicle and I couldn't see him. When I backed up I smashed right into his cycle. Of course he wanted me to stop and reimburse him for it. I told him I couldn't do anything and that I had to get these men to the hospital to give blood. He backed off and I took off with another load of prisoners to give blood. What a night! We'd done all we could and about 1:00 a.m. the lady's husband came to tell me she died. I asked him what he was going to do and he didn't have any idea, so I went to the hospital and picked up her remains in a pine box and placed it in the back of our carryall. I'm glad no official was investigating what I was doing, as it was against the law but it was the Philippines and a whole lot just gets done sometimes because it has to be done.

Off we went to Sariaya, The lady in her pine box and me driving. I left her off at the funeral parlor in Sariaya and came home to Lucena. Our house girls were scared to death to ride in our carryall after that because it had been used to haul a dead body. Their superstitions made them believe that something bad would happen to them because of this, perhaps even their own deaths.

Next was a funeral for this woman. At least her husband had a grave dug at the local cemetery but left much of the rest to me. They brought her in her pine box but with handles on the side of the casket now, which they'd rented from the local funeral parlor. However, there was one big problem with these handles; they'd been attached upside down so that someone using the handles would smash his knuckles into the casket. So the men, in the sala of their house, sought to rectify the situation by removing a few screws and reattaching the handles to the casket right side up. All the while they were doing this the poor corpse was being jostled back and forth in the casket. Then one of the ladies leaned over to the dead one and said, "Just a little patience, just a little patience." When this was finally completed I was able to proceed with the funeral service, which I performed in the Tagalog language.

Next it was off to the cemetery for the burial. Normally they would have put the dead in a cement niche built on top of the earth and probably rented for about seven years. Later, whatever remained would be scooped out of the grave and buried in a common plot, but this poor woman was assigned to the earthen lot that very day. We walked to the cemetery from their house with the men carrying the deceased in her pine box with the handles now in the correct position. Upon arrival at the burial spot I climbed up on the loose dirt and prepared for the committal, when I noticed a young man down in the gravesite looking ashen gray, which was quite a change in color for a brown skinned Filipino. He had helped dig the grave and somehow he felt that he needed to be down there again but he got scared to death that he was going to get buried too. He started clawing at one end of the grave and somehow he came out of there without help. I realized then that he had some kind of mental problem, which gave us a better understanding of the whole scenario. We got the woman buried and her husband wanted to give me their son, who was about eight years old. I wasn't sure if he feared raising the boy alone or if this was to be remuneration in some way for all we'd done for them. We were going on our home assignment in about two weeks so there was nothing more I could do right then to help care for the boy.

It was hard to leave Lucena and Sariaya as the church had just gotten going but we asked a young man to come and be the pastor who had just graduated from FEBIAS College of the Bible in Manila. He took over in an admirable way, though it was his first experience pastoring. Later our colleagues, the Leonard Tuggys came back to their church in Candelaria and also oversaw the work in Sariaya along with Pastor Baldemor from the Lucena Church.

The Lucena Baptist Church

Sariaya Baptist Church

The Lucena Choir presenting their Christmas concert

Pastor Roger & Flor Baldemor & family

# Chapter 22

## Furlough Time

Before long, our first term of missionary service was over and it was time to make preparations to go home to rest and report to our supporting churches. It had been a long time away with no more than two long distance calls from the States. Mark, now four years old, didn't remember anything about the U.S. The twins would be entering third grade in school.

Leaving the Philippines meant packing up our belongings and storing them somewhere, until we knew what our next term had in store for us. This was a huge task and we were thankful for the Filipinos who faithfully came to our aid. We had to sell some items and unfortunately had a few things stolen in the process. When an American is moving, many come to see what might be available. Consequently a great variety of people came through the house and it was impossible to keep our eyes on everyone that came. The brand new shoes I had just purchased for Mark somehow disappeared which necessitated another purchase.

The day of departure, May 29, 1969, we drove to Manila and flew to the States. We decided there would be no more sea voyages for us! We decided our port of entry would be Seattle as Steve had several relatives there. His uncle and aunt, Wesley and Lilly Lund and daughters Karen

145

and Kristi met us at the airport. They lived out on Vashon Island at the time, which necessitated taking a ferry. Uncle Wes took us shopping and each of us was the recipient of something special. The twins received a leather shoulder bag and Mark dearly loved the cowboy boots he received. He was really into playing cowboy but wore them endlessly as they were so easy to slip on and off.

We spent a few overnights with Wes and Lil and had dinner with Steve's uncle and aunt, Ed and Josie Swenson and Gene and Ray Urness. This was our first experience with jet lag. I noticed the twins fell asleep kneeling on the floor with their heads on a couch early in the evening. The next morning we were awake very early, as we had to be ready for our flight to Minneapolis where our families met us. What a thrill to meet two new little nieces, fair-haired Darla Mann, and Lori Haglund, a curly haired brunette. Darla was the only child of Hildi and Bill. Since they had lost their first two children, they were so eager for us to meet Darla. Lori was Ken and Loma's second little girl. It was great to know and enjoy them throughout the next year at home, and what a joy it was to see my "new Daddy" though he was now in a wheelchair due to arthritis and what he always called his "rheumatism." He truly was changed in every way and how grateful we were to see the evidence.

Soon after our arrival we began looking for a place to live in Minnesota or Wisconsin. Meanwhile, we were staying with Steve's parents in South Minneapolis. We scoured both states and couldn't seem to find anything within our missionary rental allowance. We were getting weary of looking when one day, Loma saw an ad in the paper with a house for sale in Crystal, Minnesota, a suburb in North Minneapolis. It was a small track home in a neighborhood that felt like home. There were people in the area that used to attend Fourth Baptist Church when I was secretary there and we knew it would not be far to the airport and main highways for traveling. I prayed, *Oh God, this seems so right for us but we have no idea how we could purchase this house. Please show us a way if it is your will.* I had a bit of an inheritance from one of my uncles but it was just a drop in the bucket compared to what we would need. Then Steve's dad, who had just retired, felt led of the Lord to give us a lump sum from his retirement so we could purchase the house. Charlotte and Phoebe, not yet married, planned to rent it while we were back on the field.

The main floor simply had a living room, kitchen, two bedrooms and a bath. The upstairs attic was paneled in knotty pine and served as a bedroom for the girls with room at one end for a sewing area. The full basement had another bathroom with a shower, a small kitchen, laundry room, and large living-dining area, which was very helpful when we had a large group to entertain. The garage was at the back with entrance from an alley. Garbage was also picked up in the alley. Apple trees, tulips, ferns, and several types of perennial flowers graced the backyard that was enclosed with a fence. It was small but adequate and we thanked God for a good place to live with friendly neighbors.

Our home in Crystal, Minnesota

Mark bidding goodbye to the twins and
neighbor girl on first day of school

Tami and Terri were now in third grade at Fair
Elementary School in Robbinsdale, just north of Crystal.
After being home schooled we were eager to see how they
would do and were relieved to find they did very well. We
were told they even had a seventh-grade level in phonics.
Mark was not in school yet so we enjoyed having him
home all day. He was blessed to have several little boys in
the neighborhood to play with. We attended Robbinsdale
Baptist Church where many former Fourth Baptist folks
were attending and we felt right at home. They also were
one of our supporting churches.

We had fifty-two supporting churches plus several
individuals to visit in one year and they stretched from
north to south and east to west across the U.S. Steve, of
course had to travel to the more distant places alone and
I had many speaking engagements in the Minnesota and
Wisconsin area.

A pleasant surprise came one day when Herb Hazzard said the negatives to our wedding pictures had been found and he had gotten them printed. We realized again, God's hand in this incident. If we had them before, they doubtless would have been in the shed with the things that burned. In reality, God had spared them after all.

# Chapter 23

## *"Daddy, Come Quick"*

In the cold month of January I began to feel weak and couldn't understand why. One morning as the girls were getting ready for school, I fainted in the bathroom. They immediately called out, "Daddy, come quick, Mommy has fainted." I was lying behind the door and Steve wasn't able to get to me. Finally he tried to lead me to the bedroom and I fainted again on the bedroom floor. He was scared to death and he had just gotten home in the wee hours of the morning from a long drive. He tends to have low blood pressure and perhaps that, along with tiredness, and fear, caused him to faint and land in a pile of Legos Mark had left on his bedroom floor. I then came to and couldn't figure out what was happening as the kids were saying, "Now Daddy's doing it." I wondered if there was monoxide poisoning in the house so I instructed the kids to open the doors and go and get our neighbor lady. She was the nervous type and didn't know what to do but the gas company was called and it was proven that there was no monoxide gas in the house. The poor kids were freezing by the open doors, as it was about forty degrees below zero that morning. Steve's folks came quickly and his mom said they should get me to their family doctor, as I had no color in my skin, even in my hands and feet. We followed their advice and the doctor thought I might have an inner ear infection from a recent cold virus and sent me home with some medicine.

However, I didn't regain strength or color so we headed to Wisconsin the next day to the doctor that delivered Mark. He took one look and said, "Young Lady, I think you are bleeding from an ulcer," so I was placed in the hospital in Baldwin. They kept watching my condition and soon I had lost more blood. Because that hospital didn't have my blood type, I was sent by ambulance to Ramsey Hospital in St. Paul, Minnesota. Steve wasn't able to be with me in the ambulance but followed in our old Ford Falcon. I was so weak, I wondered if I'd live to see him again. I kept feeling guilty because I couldn't witness to the man in the ambulance but I was unable to.

The first thing they did was to pump my stomach, and then started blood transfusions. My veins had collapsed so they had to make an incision in order to get blood into me. I spent several days in the hospital where I was put through many exploratory tests and was placed on a special diet. I was so weak I couldn't talk to my visitors. I remember telling Steve if I didn't make it he had to promise me he would find a good mommy for the kids. He, of course, didn't want to hear any of that. It was a frightening time for all of us.

Through all of the procedures, they could not locate the ulcer. It wasn't in the stomach as thought. I had lost over half my blood so a plea went out for blood donations. I praise God for the many people, including Pastor McCormick of Robbinsdale Baptist who donated blood for me. Finally the day came when I could leave the hospital. However, the kids had a very bad virus, nigh unto pneumonia, therefore, the doctor would not allow me to go home right away. I was able to go to Ken and Loma's where I stayed another week. At least I could talk to the kids by phone. They were so sick and eventually

Grandma Sonmor who stayed with them got pneumonia and had to be hospitalized. She had a bad heart and we were very concerned about her. While at Ken and Loma's, I found I had a bladder or urinary tract infection due to being catheterized so I had to be treated for that. Finally the day came when I could really go home. The kids had made "welcome home" signs and notes for me that were so precious. Needless to say, we were very happy to be together again. God, not man, rules over all. It was never determined where the source of the bleeding was, but doctors have said it could have been caused by a dysentery I had in the Philippines that bled through an intestine. I guess we will never know but God was once again faithful. What would we ever do without Him?

While home on furlough, we had the privilege of having Pastor Roger Baldemor, from Lucena, come to the States and stay in our home. What a joy to introduce him to our families and some of our churches. He particularly appreciated going to the farm in Wisconsin where he enjoyed the country scenery and had the thrill of driving the riding lawn mower.

# Chapter 24

## Joy and Sorrow

We took Tami and Terri out of school around Easter that year and travelled to the East Coast where we had many supporting churches. That was the only time we would have been able to meet the supporters in the East. The kids were able to see some of the historical sites in the area, which helped them learn a bit more of our country's history. We were so thankful God gave us that time together as we have never been able to do that again.

As spring arrived, we knew we had to do some repairs on the window frames of the house. While Steve worked we listened to a Christian radio station. Suddenly a shocking announcement was made. A missionary friend with another mission had been murdered in Lucena City, Philippines. This missionary worked to the south of us and would often drive his motorcyle to our house and leave it there while he took a bus to Manila. We couldn't believe our ears. I believe the man who shot him was the highest-ranking police officer and he was intoxicated. The missionary's companion, a Filipino pastor, who was driving the car, was passing through Barrio Red-V, which was very close to where we lived while in Lucena City. The police officer and one of his lieutenants were driving through the same barrio at a very slow rate of speed, so the pastor decided to overtake them. In the mind of the police officer, this was very egregious and he and his companion overtook the missionary's car and pulled them over. They prepared to beat the missionary, so he cupped his hands over his face to shield his eyes and face from serious damage. However, since the police and his lieutenant were drunk, they interpreted this as an attempt to fight them. The policeman then ordered his companion to shoot the missionary with his 45 caliber side arm and commanded him in the Tagalog language with "patayin mo siya," which means, "kill him," which he, in actuality, did for our friend died enroute to the provincial hospital about two miles away. The missionary's Filipino pastor, and driver on this occasion, was so badly affected by this that it has limited his ability to minister to this very day.

The missionary was dead and there was a trial some months later involving the police officer and his lieutenant. Everyone hoped justice would be done but because the chief was appointed by President Marcos, the accused were all exonerated and cleared of charges.

We have grieved for this missionary family and his Filipino companion. How sad that in a very clear case of injustice no one was able to get redress for a crime committed by those who had sworn to uphold the law. Especially bothered was our dear pastor friend, Rogelio Baldemor who pastored our Conservative Baptist Church located about a half mile from the scene of the shooting and on the same road. One day when Pastor Baldemor was reading in the Psalms, he came across Psalm 55:23b, which says, "Bloodthirsty and deceitful men shall not live out half their days." He said, "This is the answer to this terrible injustice." In fact he shared this with his deacons and declared that this police officer in Lucena would be dead in a little while.

This man was involved in the murders of several men in Lucena prior to this incident, and of course had made many enemies in the process. One evening he was sitting in his car waiting for a relative when a former fellow officer, who had issues to settle with him, approached him giving the evening greeting, "Magandang Gabi, Po," (Good evening, Sir) and then turned his pistol on him filling him full of bullets until he died while seated in his car. God's Word had been fulfilled just as Pastor Baldemor said.

Prior to our return to the Philippines, our family, Charlotte, and Ken and Loma's family, took a camping trip to Colorado. We did some backpacking and saw sights around Ouray, Colorado Springs, and the Royal Gorge. It was a time that our kids and their cousins will always remember.

Upon our arrival back to Minneapolis, we expected the daily call from my dad. He called every day to talk to each of the kids. Since he hadn't called, I thought I'd better call and let him know we were back, however, I got no answer. I thought perhaps he was in the cafeteria eating lunch or something. He was living in an assisted living apartment complex in South Minneapolis. Since I didn't get an answer, we decided to go and check on him. As we got ready to leave, we received a call from a policeman asking us to come as it appeared Dad had passed away late the day before or during the night and they needed a family member to identify him. We found him slumped in his hallway with a smile on his face. Though it was a sad time, we had peace. We enjoyed him so much during that year and we knew now my dear mom knew her prayers were answered as he was in heaven with her at the age of seventy-three. He was buried July 16, 1970, next to Mom in Hastings, Minnesota. We were so thankful we were still at home during this time. Due to his poor health, we knew we would never have seen him again after this furlough. God's timing is always perfect.

God gave us so many good times with family during that year as we all lived relatively close to one another. Our picnic table under the apple trees became a favorite gathering place. God knew what we needed for that year of furlough and soon it would be over.

Just prior to leaving for the Philippines, I realized I was pregnant again. We were definitely not prepared for this. We quickly set about purchasing supplies for a new baby as well as maternity clothes. This meant more things to pack and get sent off to the Philippines. It seems we could never do things in any easy, relaxed fashion. Something unexpected often came up to surprise us.

To add to unexpected situations, we got a phone call from the field chairman asking us to consider going to a new place this term. It was a place called Makati, known as the Wall Street area of the Philippines. Makati was a place with many specialty shops, business organizations, and many gated communities called "villages" where the wealthiest people in the country lived. We were a bit scared and frightened to work with the millionaire class. We felt so at home in Lucena and loved the people there but we committed to pray about it. We had come to realize that whatever God has for us is of His choosing and is always best.

This new location also necessitated getting a different vehicle than a carryall. One of our supporters in South Dakota had a car dealership and offered us a good price on a new Pontiac Catalina. We weren't sure about this fancy looking car but inquired of the field chairman who gave us the word to go ahead. It seemed it would fit in well in the Makati work. We didn't realize at the time how important that car would be in our work but God knew. He always does.

What was God going to do with us during this term? We couldn't help but give Him praise for all He had done

for us on this furlough with its many trials but we saw
His hand and perfect timing in everything and knew He
would take care of us and see us through as He had our
first term. We found ourselves having hearts filled with
great anticipation as we flew to San Francisco and on to
Tokyo, our first stop.

# Chapter 25

*Tokyo*

We left Minneapolis on August 7, 1970, for our second term of missionary service. Prior to our departure, we had a special time with family at Hildi and Bill's farm in Princeton, Minnesota, as well as a family breakfast at our home the day of our departure. Many friends came by to pray and wish us well. We drove our new Pontiac to the West Coast, staying in a motel in Glen Ullin, North Dakota, the first day and then on to Powell, Wyoming, where we renewed friendships and spoke on Sunday at First Baptist Church. After the evening service the church loaded us up with gifts they had set aside for us for our next term of service. Steve then took an overnight fishing trip with some of the men while the kids and I stayed at our friends, the Carter's. We left that afternoon, driving through Yellowstone Park and on into Idaho driving all night with cat naps now and then. We only stopped for gas and groceries to eat in the car.

I recall seeing a clever sign, "Lost? Keep going, you're making good time anyway." A little humor along the way was welcomed. We stayed in a Nevada motel that night where we were happy to get a bath after our days of traveling.

On August 12th we arrived at "Home of Peace" where we unloaded our supplies to be shipped and I packed two more barrels. We called our friends, Joe and Florence Leach who were expecting us. The following day, Steve worked all day making more crates for our supplies. Florence took the twins and me shopping to buy shoes for them and the rest of the day was spent getting more organized with the last-minute packing.

We left San Francisco on August 14, 1970, flying to Anchorage, Alaska. There we met a fellow from Anoka, Minnesota, who was going to New Guinea. We were surprised that he knew Glady and Tom. The kids were too tired to eat dinner and slept till we got to Tokyo where we arrived at 6:00 a.m. our time but about 10:00 p.m. Tokyo time. We had no problem in customs and Marty and Arlene Shaw, our fellow missionary friends, were there to meet us and drove us to their home. We got the kids to bed while Steve and I talked with Marty and Arlene till about 1:30 am. There was so much news to catch up with regarding their first term there in Japan. Marty had attended Northwestern College and was from Mound, Minnesota. We saw them off at the airport the day they left for Japan.

While at the Shaws we attended Calvary Baptist Church on a military base. The Shaws worked with the Christian Servicemen Center in Tokyo. We sang a duet at the church and later went out for Chinese food. At night following the evening service, we were able to observe a Japanese Obong Festival where the people call out for the dead and bring food for their spirits. They dress up in weird costumes and dance to attract attention. It was a picture of the hopelessness of those who don't know Christ as Savior.

The following day Steve and Marty took Mark and their son, Marty Jr., shopping and Tami, Terri and I accompanied Arlene to downtown Tokyo. It took four train rides to get there. We purchased a few mementoes, then took the trains back home. I began to feel some cramping at night. The following morning, I continued to have cramping and passed a blood clot. Marty called the Seventh Day Adventist Hospital and made arrangements for me to have an exam. Steve called Vern Carvey, our legal representative, in the Philippines to let them know we would not be arriving as planned. They were very surprised, as we had not informed anyone there that I was expecting. I was given some injections for pain but the strong contractions continued.

Steve brought me a lovely bouquet of roses and stayed with me all day except for an occasional jaunt down the street. Very little English is spoken in Japan; consequently he had quite a time making the purchase. Apparently pointing was his main method of communication. A little Japanese lady came into my room to clean and with a very sweet expression on her face, shook her head sadly and said, "No more baby." The doctor then explained that I had miscarried the baby and prayed for me before doing a D and C. We are not sure of the cause but I knew I didn't have the normal feelings of pregnancy for quite a while so I wondered if the baby had died before we even got to Tokyo. Whatever the case, I was thankful to be in a place where I was given good care. God provided a doctor who prayed for me and following my release from the hospital I was in the presence of friends. The sadness of losing the baby didn't really hit me until a week or so later in Manila.

Upon arriving at the Shaws we found that Tami and Terri had been at Vacation Bible School for the day and had the privilege of touring the Lipton Tea Company. Mark stayed at Shaws playing with Marty, Jr. and drawing pictures, which was his chief hobby. The twins went another day to Bible School and this time they had a tour of the Coca Cola plant. That night we called the Philippines to let them know our arrival time the next day.

# Chapter 26

## *Home Life in Makati*

As we arrived in Manila on August 21, 1970, we were taken from the airport directly to the mission guesthouse where we stayed for several weeks while looking for a home to rent in Makati. Art and Sonia Beals had worked in this area previously but had recently resigned to pursue ministry in the States. They lived in San Lorenzo Village, one of the many gated communities in Makati. We looked in that area first and eventually found the home that we would live in for the next four years. However, our children would have to start school at Faith Academy while we were still at the guesthouse as it took time to get all of the paperwork done and bring our possessions from Lucena to Makati.

Tami and Terri were now in fourth grade and Mark was beginning kindergarten. They were so excited but a little apprehensive. However, the girls met some friends they knew from kindergarten that helped them feel at home. They were put in separate classrooms just as they were in the States. After teaching them myself, I could understand the advantage in that as they were very competitive and there would sometimes be big tears if one did better than the other. Fortunately, that was not a one-sided affair. They took turns "besting" one another. Terri had Joy Limburg, one of our own missionaries as her teacher and Tami had a teacher named Vera Ewoldt who was with the Evangelical Free Church mission. Both were outstanding teachers and the girls enjoyed school and did very well. Mark didn't know anyone in his class but really liked his teacher and soon got acquainted with his classmates. He had Wednesdays off from school just as the girls did when they were in kindergarten.

The kids rode the Faith Academy bus to school. Their bus stop was very convenient, just around the corner of our block. We were thankful Mark had his older sisters to look after him on the bus. Our home in San Lorenzo was a busy place and God provided an ideal house for the many activities we'd be involved in. The large screened porch in the front was used for youth meetings, women's meetings, and fun times for the kids and their friends. Large sliding glass doors closed off the porch at night and opened into a large living-dining room combination and a kitchen adjacent to the dining room. From the living room we stepped up to a higher level hallway leading to three bedrooms and two baths. We divided the middle bedroom into a study for Steve and a bedroom for Mark. The maids' quarters were at the back of the house with an outside entrance. The laundry area was located on one side of the house with an outside entrance. The carport at the front was next to the porch entrance.

One of the girls in front of the Makati house

A cement wall surrounded the front and back yards where there was grass, flowering trees and shrubs. We especially appreciated the pili nut tree in the front yard, as it was difficult to find nuts in the Philippines. Mark also enjoyed climbing it, as it was easy and safe.

Speaking of nuts, one missionary asked her housegirl to make cookies and make them the size of walnuts. The finished project was a huge cookie the size of a coconut—the only nut she was familiar with.

The neighborhood was truly an international community. We had Japanese neighbors on one side of us, Swedes on the other side, Germans directly across the street, Afghans further down the street, as well as Americans, Filipinos and Spanish. A block or so away we had Norwegians. Each morning I could view from our bedroom window, the Japanese neighbor faithfully doing his calisthenics. We knew they were a very disciplined people.

Mark played with the Swedish boys, Magnus, Stephan, and Hokan most and they created what they called "The Viking's Club" and dressed up with all the typical Viking shields, swords, and hats. Their father was with the World Health Organization and we had great times with all the family. They invited us to a Swedish smorgasbord one Christmas Eve. I readily understood my Swedish heritage and the food we used to have in my family as we too always had a smorgasbord type of meal on Christmas Eve with pickled herring, Swedish meatballs, and many different breads, pastries and cheese. They invited a blond girl dressed as a Santa Lucia wearing a lingonberry wreath on her head and the boys wore tall hats and passed out cookies to all. They had invited the Norwegians and people from other countries. The subject eventually went to politics and we were shocked to hear most of them speak of America as an imperialistic nation desiring to take over the world. We shared our views but they didn't seem to believe us. We realized how much our worldview is influenced by the news and propaganda we hear and much of it is inaccurate.

The "Viking's Club"

Tami and Terri were so happy to meet the Parkman twins who lived very close to us in our village. Olivia and Laura's parents were Southern Baptist missionaries. Our twins were several years younger but they really enjoyed each other, riding the same school bus. They created a stand with a sign, "Twins Club" and sold calamansi juice, the next thing to lemonade. They did a lot of things together.

Mark became a member of Cub Scouts through Faith Academy and loved working on his badges. It provided some good discipline for him and it was something for him to feel a part of.

Mark loved cub scouts

An American family with the U.S. Air Force lived down our street and we became well acquainted with them as well. They had four children, a boy a little older than Mark, a daughter Mark's age, a younger boy, and a baby boy about two. If Mark wasn't playing with the Swedish boys he was playing with these children. We had become quite good friends while they were in Makati. Later they were placed back in the States, but we saw God work in their lives to see them come to Christ and be active in the church. God was so good in providing good and helpful neighbors.

Tami and Terri were fortunate to inherit Aunt Glady's clarinet (Clarabelle) and Steve's cousin Sylvia's clarinet, which we brought with us to the Philippines. They joined the band at Faith Academy and did very well, playing first and second chair. Mark, even in kindergarten, excelled in art and that talent followed him on into his adult life into his profession. As he progressed in school at Faith

Academy, he got excellent training as they had a great art program. He was able, at a young age, to identify the works of most of the famous artists. There were many outstanding artists in Manila and whenever possible we took Mark to watch them paint. This was a special treat for him.

The girls always enjoyed playing basketball after school so Steve put up a hoop on the carport just as he had in Lucena. Eventually they got uniforms and played on the San Lorenzo team in our village. They were the shortest players but very fast and clever. They felt challenged to do something well that was considered only for those who were tall. They never reached more than four feet eleven inches even as adults. Filipinos are generally small but all of the girls on the team were taller than they. Tall girls were very frustrated with them as they were so difficult to guard. Their part on this team provided an outlet for us in our community and opened doors to get to know people. Mark eventually joined them at the hoop but he knew at this age he couldn't compete. In later years he too became active in that sport but at this time he was content to go to his room and draw. Steve wondered at times about the interests of our kids. He would often ask, "Why do I have girls that come home and want to play basketball and a boy who wants to sit in his room and draw?" However, a closer look at Mark's drawings revealed he was drawing tanks, planes, bombs going off and all things boys were interested in. We saw in later years God had a perfect plan he was putting together even in their tender years.

Steve would often go to the village park at night and play basketball just to get to know the guys that would be there. One night he met a tall, husky Filipino guy who had been on drugs. He got a chance to talk to him about salvation. His parents wouldn't allow him to come home till he was free of his addiction. Steve brought him home to our house where he took over Mark's room for a night. Steve was able to get this guy into a hospital and we continued to have contact with his family. He claimed to receive the Lord as his Savior. We were invited into their home and his mother took me to a special event at the Cultural Center in Manila. She was a very classy lady who owned a shop for women that included a woodcarver who could carve your facial image if you chose to have it done. She specialized in classic native dresses and furniture. One photograph section of a Sunday paper was devoted to showing her shop and its wares. She gave me a native dress as a gift and I wore this for certain Philippine presentations in the States.

We had several other gated villages in Makati where other missionaries lived. Many of them had children at Faith Academy so our kids got to know them at school as well as riding the school bus. We became good friends with Boyd and Donna Lyons, Bible Baptist missionaries, while we attended language school together. They also moved to Makati and lived in Bel Aire Village, about a mile or so away. Our kids had gotten acquainted quite well during that time. We were so fortunate to have friends that we were intimately acquainted with in close proximity. Donna and I would often shop together and our families went to the beach together a few times. We were able to encourage each other in hard times and learn together through some of the difficult circumstances we faced, whether it was health issues or cultural problems.

All three of our kids took piano from a Southern Baptist missionary in that village as well. I found they did so much better when they had someone other than their mother for a teacher. It was a greater challenge to practice and she was an excellent teacher. As Mark got older, he began to learn to play the trumpet, which we had purchased on furlough.

Oftentimes we had missionary kids, who were boarding students, come for a weekend. It was a pleasant change for these kids to be in a home again and it also made it possible for our kids to get to know them better by having more time with them.

Our children mingled freely with the Filipino kids in the church and often spent the night in each other's homes. The twins even went to the church camp out in the province. Tami got very sick, however, and had we known we would have gone and brought them home. She had dysentery so severe she had to be isolated from the other campers. We felt so bad for her. The girls were baptized with other young people from the Makati church in our Quezon City Church. They were about nine years old at the time.

During our first year in San Lorenzo Village, we experienced a very serious typhoon. Our entire front yard was like a jungle with trees and bushes destroyed. In some ways it was a blessing as there were far too many bushes growing up entangled together. We were able to thin it out which improved the looks of the yard and gave us a better view of the neighborhood. Faith Academy, however, did not fare so well. The roof had blown off several buildings; the new gym, library, and many classrooms were damaged. Therefore, the school had to be closed temporarily. Many of the books were brought to our front porch to dry out and we had to keep flipping the pages often so they wouldn't be ruined. Classes were held at Union Church in Makati (United Church of Christ) and many of us had to take boarding students into our homes until they could repair all the damage. We thank God for many willing hearts and hands that pitched in and eventually brought the school back to normal.

Some of the typhoon damage at Faith Academy

Some of the missionaries who had kids in boarding school picked up their kids at our home on Fridays. They would ride the Makati bus and come to our house. We always enjoyed these brief encounters each week; otherwise we would have had no connection with them for long periods of time. Truly it was a busy household. I think it was the Norwegian neighbors that referred to our house as the one where something was always happening. We were also closest to the airport so when missionaries were coming from another field, they would invariably stop briefly before heading to their final destination.

God definitely provided the right house for that time in our lives. At one point the owner wanted to raise the rent and the mission felt it was too high. We looked at many places for over a month but couldn't find a better place convenient to our work. The mission agreed we should stay put, and we know God wanted us to remain there for the rest of our term for there were people we met and ministered to that would not have been possible if we were not in that location.

# Chapter 27

*Makati Ministry*

A church had already begun in Makati under the previous missionary with a rented air-conditioned auditorium on the eighth floor of the Comtrust Bank building that had comfortable theater seats and a curtained elevated stage equipped with a piano and podium. This was located on Ayala Avenue, often referred to as the Wall Street of the Philippines. This area was the location of many large businesses and not far from the Makati Commercial Center that had many elite shops, the Intercontinental Hotel and fancy restaurants.

When we started working in Makati we had a lot of organizational work to do such as getting a deacon board elected and operating as well as Sunday School classes and teachers prepared. Eventually a choir, women's meetings, and youth ministry began. My duties included preparing the church bulletin for each week by means of an old-fashioned mimeograph, as well as preparing for my own Sunday School class and special music for each week. I often think how much easier some of these things would have been and how much more attractive if we would have had computers at that time. How time changes things! We also had opening exercises for Sunday School that we referred to as "Family Time." This was designed to encourage people to be on time; hence this had to be something they were looking forward to. For a time I did this using flannel graph lessons and songs. I also played the piano.

Later we were privileged to have Vera Ewoldt, Tami's fourth grade teacher at Faith Academy join our fellowship. Being a master storyteller she made this time on Sunday morning come alive. Her use of drama, object lessons, puppets, and elements of surprise was very impressive in relating the truth of God's Word to the people. She helped me with the young people and women's ministry as well. Vera is about six feet tall, a foot taller than me so we quickly became known as Mutt and Jeff.

On one occasion we dressed up as clowns for a Halloween party. Her clown suit accentuated her height with stripes in vertical position while mine was stripes in horizontal position. Filipinos really enjoyed dressing up for Halloween. One family, particularly, had a mom who was a make-up artist and her children were totally unrecognizable at our Halloween parties. We tried to make this holiday one that showed the difference between the evil and death surrounding that day and the hope that we have in Christ. November first, "All Saints Day" is a special day of celebration in the Philippines as people visit the graves of their loved ones and bring them food. Instead we seek to bring them joy in knowing the hope we have as Christians. "To be absent from the body and to be present with the Lord" (2 Corinthians 5:8b).

We trained the choir to sing a cantata for Easter and Christmas and presented these to a few other churches in the Manila area as well. The children also presented special programs at Christmas. I was able to again use the program I wrote for the Dallas Christian Day School but this time it was presented in English. Our people were from various locations in the Philippines and spoke several different dialects. Japanese and Spanish folks were also a part of our congregation; therefore, English was the best choice.

The Makati Choir

Along with our church ministries, both Steve and I taught at our Conservative Baptist Bible College located near Phil-Am Life where we lived when we first arrived. It was held in Capitol City Baptist Church. Steve was a Bible instructor and I taught music theory and worked with a small singing group. We both enjoyed this ministry a great deal.

There were other duties within our mission at large, such as serving on various committees. Steve served as secretary for the mission for a time and reported and took notes at our annual conferences. All of our missionaries in the Philippines would gather together for a week of Field Conference each year and discuss policies, strategies, procedures, financial matters, and about everything you can think of. We usually had a special Bible teacher share spiritual truth with us as adults, and someone to teach the children as well.

We closed the conference with a banquet and special program that inspired and encouraged us as we returned to our individual ministries.

Clark Air Base was north of Manila and we were occasionally called on to minister to servicemen there. Steve spoke and together we presented music. Subic Naval Base was farther north and we were invited to minister there while on vacation in Baguio but Mark got very sick with dysentery and we were unable to go. Faith Academy's basketball team played the schools at Subic and Clark as well as other teams in the Far East. That was quite an experience for these missionary kids. When Tami and Terri were a little older they went to Clark on the Faith Academy bus when our basketball team played at Clark. They enjoyed that so much as they were able to buy stateside candy or gum and ration it out over a period of days making it last as long as possible. We had a couple guys from the servicemen's center that came to visit us from time to time and would bring oranges and other things that we could not get in our supermarkets. They were Christian guys who were a great blessing to us. They also enjoyed getting off the base and being in a home.

Our churches were organized in groups of provinces for fellowship. We were now in the Camapariza group made up of the churches in Cavite, Manila, Pampanga, and Rizal provinces. I was a part of the Women's organization and along with the Filipino leaders wrote the by-laws and constitution for the Camapariza Women's fellowship. My days with the Dallas Seminary Wives' Fellowship proved to be of help in organizing and advising this group in the Philippines. I remember several outstanding meetings, but the one I recall the most was on top of the PAL Airlines building. Our theme was "The Meeting in the Air" and our speaker, Mary Ann Samms, one of our own missionaries told of her experience as a trapeze artist prior to her missionary life. A ladies' trio sang "The Meeting in the Air" and other related songs.

Often we had missionary speakers from other countries that were coming through Manila. God worked in many ways with the hearts of women in the Philippines.

With women in our area, I had a sewing class. This was aimed at reaching women outside of the church by providing them with information that all women needed as well as providing fellowship. There is very little ready-made clothing in the Philippines; consequently, most Filipinos go to a tailor or modista (female seamstress) to have their clothing made. These modistas and tailors were able to simply look at a picture and create what was desired. Patterns for sewing your own clothes were not available, therefore, this class provided information on how to measure themselves or others and draw up their own patterns according to the style they desired. We secured a special teacher who was trained in this technique. The class also included a short devotional time emphasizing the importance of becoming a godly woman.

As a wife I did most of the cooking in our home although occasionally I had a house girl who was trained to do quite well at it and would always help with the basics. Other duties included office and secretarial work. We had what seemed like tons of correspondence to our churches and the home office in the States. I took shorthand as Steve dictated letters and at times wrote them myself. I remember several occasions when I typed at least fifty letters in one day. For our families, I made carbon copies of one letter that was sent to all of them. There were many records to keep concerning other ministries under our supervision, like smaller churches with a national pastor, literature and work funds. Steve of course met with these workers and I would take care of the records, some of which were financial and others required correspondence. On one occasion the church under our supervision asked me to come and speak on the family altar. It was primarily a Tagalog congregation so I tried my best in Tagalog but had to resort to English for certain words.

Financial records were required for funds that were designated for certain aspects of the work. How we dreaded these "green sheets." We had to be sure everything balanced and was sent in at a definite time. There were also medical records for the home office as well as periodic prayer letters and annual reports.

Alien registration forms and driver's licenses had to be kept current. These things are not exciting to write about but hopefully it will enlighten folks about some of the responsibilities of missionaries that they may not be aware of. They consume many hours, yet are necessary for the work.

Camping was a great ministry throughout our mission in the Philippines. There were youth camps where we participated in music and teaching. We also had retreats for the women. During our first year in Makati, the Campariza women had a very special retreat in a rural area. A family offered their large, bamboo vacation house for our use. The women brought sleeping bags, food and other supplies. The program included music, games, special speakers, testimonies, fellowship and election of officers. I think my predominant memory of that retreat was the women giggling at night when one woman seemed to be answering the other with her snoring. I also remember getting stuck in the mud while driving to the location with my bunch of ladies. Most prominent in my mind though was the testimony of one of our ladies who had just recently come to know Christ as her Savior.

Missionary, Alice Benson, leading a fun time at our retreat

Steve had a host of Bible studies in various homes, which was the primary means of evangelism. He was either teaching a Bible study or calling on homes to start a new one. He also did a great deal of counseling. We never could have imagined some of the folks who came for that purpose. There were drug addicts, homosexuals, marriage problems, and spiritual problems both inside and outside of the church. If it were not for privacy issues, we could share more openly, however, we will be sharing some of the exciting things God has done in some individuals in a coming chapter entitled, "Trophies of Grace."

While we were in Makati, we had the privilege to meet the former commander of the first air fleet of the Japanese Imperial Navy who led the attack on Pearl Harbor in 1941. Eleven years later he was led to Christ through a former American prisoner of war, who had returned to Japan as a missionary. Mitsuo Fuchida, who became an ambassador of peace, spoke at Capital City Baptist Church where we heard him and got his picture and personal autograph. He related that his view of life was now revolutionized, saying, "Now I am convinced that the way for Japan is neither left with Communism nor right with Imperialism. I believe that the only answer to peace . . . is Jesus Christ." Truly that is the answer for all people. Filipino Christians were touched with his message for there had been deep animosity in their hearts toward the Japanese, as many had suffered severely at their hands.

News came in March 1974, while we were in Makati, that Lieutenant Hiroo Onoda of the Japanese Imperial Army, stationed in the Philippines, was not aware that the war had ended thirty years before. Because he was given orders to stay and fight, he dismissed the many attempts that had been made to track him down. He thought these were a means of trickery or propaganda from the enemy. Japanese soldiers were very loyal to their commanders, hence his commander had to come to the Philippines to officially rescind his order, and tell him he was relieved of his duty. (Note of interest: As I began to relate this incident one evening, I had to depend on my memory and my husband's recollection. The very next morning, a friend e-mailed a copy of *The Daily Bread* for that day, and all of the information including the name of the soldier was there. God knew I needed some improvement on this story even though I hadn't asked. I love His surprises.)

We were grateful for the work God did in our Makati Church, where Filipinos and Japanese served side-by-side and learned to love one another through the Gospel message.

# Chapter 28

## Many and Varied Calamities

Makati, which became our home from 1971-1974, provided many and varied experiences, therefore, the events in this chapter are more topical, not necessarily in chronological order.

We soon realized that superstition existed not only in the province, but it was here as well. There were fears of even talking about death for fear if one did, they would be the next person to die. There were other fears about going to bed with wet hair or riding in a vehicle that carried someone who died as it may also cause death.

There were also superstitions surrounding various religious proceedings. Catholicism had many pagan practices that we do not see in America. These centered predominately on the Good Friday-Easter season. It was not uncommon to see men carrying crosses for many miles and later would hang on the cross to atone for their sins. Then there were the Flagelantes who would beat their backs with whips to raise the flesh followed by beating themselves with a board embedded with razors. This would cause them to bleed thereby atoning for their sin. To add to their suffering, they would immerse their wounds in the salt water of the sea. Also in the Catholic faith were many processions especially during Fiesta times. Often they would have a carved image of the

Virgin Mary in the parade with someone operating the image from inside to make it appear as though she was moving, as Mary is highly honored of course. One of the most well known images is the "Black Christ," a carved image painted black. It is believed that this image has special power to give blessings to all who kiss it. So many have kissed the hand that it is almost worn away but as one doctor told Steve, those who kissed the image would supposedly not get sick because of the special power this image possessed. Filipinos revere this image highly.

The cults have also found their way into the Philippines, many of which came from the States as missionaries. A very visible, local cult is the Iglesia ni Cristo (Church of Christ) that does not recognize Christ as God and is predominately a political organization, as all of their congregations vote as one during governmental elections.

I have already alluded in a previous chapter to our interactions with drug addiction in Makati and literally it was everywhere but we definitely saw more of it in the larger cities. There were also the sexual sins like adultery, homosexuality, and rape. It was not uncommon to find many men had a secret "number two wife" with whom he raised a second family. Of course this led to jealousy, pain, and chaos when discovered. There is no divorce allowed in the Philippines, which would be ideal if all people lived as they should, but this caused its own unique emotional pain within the family structure as was seen by these secretive wives and children. Both families suffered as a result.

One would think there might not be as much poverty in a wealthy place like Makati, but in certain areas, it was very plentiful. This led to thievery and brawls as well. In the poorer areas, the people often felt their trials would be over if their physical needs were supplied, therefore, that desire superseded the desire to seek spiritual help or even recognize their need. In Makati, however, we found many who had it all physically were dissatisfied in life due to family schisms, business fraud, drugs, or any number of problems. Many times it was these issues that brought them to their need of salvation for nothing else could satisfy their troubled hearts.

For years there has been corruption in the political arena and we experienced a great deal of that. President Ferdinand Marcos was in power the entire time we were there. As is often the case with leaders, he started out well doing some very good things for the country, however, as time went on he became more and more corrupt. As a result there was a spirit of revolt developing in the country. One day while driving from the province, to Manila, we noticed all was quiet with little or no traffic on the highways nor could we get our car radio to work, which was strange. When we arrived home later, we were informed that the president had declared martial law, shut down all public communication and instituted curfews until further notice. We also got word from our fellow missionaries that if things got worse, there was an evacuation plan for all of us to meet at Faith Academy where the U.S. Air Force would take us out of the country. That is the closest we came to war, however, there were many smaller uprisings throughout our time in the Philippines.

Along with cultural and political challenges, there were the natural calamities due to the tropical storms, which brought floods, heavy winds and landslides. In Makati during one typhoon we saw our neighbor's metal roof flying down the road, which was very dangerous if it had hit someone. We heard of people having their head sliced off in such a situation. One night we were awakened by sirens in the wee hours of the morning and found our neighbor's house was burning. I don't recall if it was struck by lightning or what caused the fire but there was not much sleep that night. Typhoons brought other problems like causing the electricity to be cut off resulting also in no water in our homes. We were always amazed that a country with water all around it had such shortages of drinking water. As a result of no water, there were fights at the public places wherever water was available. We of course had no refrigeration or air-conditioning. We tried to buy ice for our ice chests to protect our food but often ended up with spoiled food that had to be discarded. These times without electricity would sometimes last a week or more. We still marvel how God took care of us during that time.

Earthquakes were very prevalent and would sometimes wake us in the night with the house moving or shaking. Light fixtures would sway and that feeling of vertigo would set in. This happened one night at a home Bible study. We were on the second floor of an apartment building and wondered whether to stay put or leave the building. It was something we never got accustomed to in spite of their frequency.

# Chapter 29

## *Medical Mishaps*

Soon after our arrival in Makati, we experienced some health issues. Mark had just gotten adjusted to kindergarten and he woke up with pain and vomiting. It kept on the next day so we took him to the Makati Medical Center where it was decided it was appendicitis. He had the appendectomy and spent several days in the hospital. Steve and I will never forget watching the nurses lead little Mark away to the operating room on the gurney. He looked so small and helpless. I'm sure many a parent can identify with that pain but it was a new experience for us.

Shortly after Mark was back home, we got a note from the school nurse that Tami had a seizure during P.E. class one day. We had a similar note another day, saying Terri had one too. We couldn't imagine what had happened to them. They seemed all right to us but we did notice all three of our kids had swollen cheeks. We wondered about mumps but they didn't get real large and they themselves seemed to feel pretty well. Soon Terri was out riding her bike in the heat and she rushed in the house and ran to me while I was talking on the phone, and collapsed at my feet. I didn't know if it was a seizure or if she had just fainted as to me it looked like she was trying to come to. We had no choice but to seek medical help. As usual our American doctor was back in the States so we had to depend on local doctors. One doctor thought we needed to see a neurologist and recommended one he thought to be very reputable. We made an appointment that happened to be on my birthday. I was so nervous and fearful and of course prayed much that God would give strength and wisdom in this great difficulty but I admit I took a Valium pill that was available over the counter there. I couldn't bear to see my girls going through this scary thing. Yet I realized our God knew exactly what the problem was.

The first thing the neurologist did was to have them lie down and breathe in and out as fast as they could. Soon Tami was "out." I wasn't surprised, as I had heard this could cause one to faint and she wasn't having any strange movements. She was one who always tried to do everything right and oftentimes would go overboard which I think she did in this case. He took some other tests and said they both had epilepsy and prescribed the usual epilepsy drugs. We could not believe this. It was a scary situation to even send them to school again but they did all right.

However, we were still concerned about their swollen glands. Soon Dr. Dill, our American doctor was back so we took them to him for an examination. He informed us that a bunch of missionary kids from Faith Academy came to him who had mononucleosis and asked me to describe what I saw in the supposed seizures. He said nothing in their exam nor my description showed that they had epilepsy. Because the girls were small and had small blood vessels, Dr. Dill said they could faint easily when under stress of heat and/or heavy exercise. He told us to take them off the medicine, as it was bad for them to take it. He also asked more about Mark's appendicitis and said he felt they had all had mono, which often affects the spleen and that is very near the appendix. He wondered about the validity of Mark's surgery as to whether or not he needed it. I did notice, the doctor who did the surgery never showed us the appendix or told us anything about it. It has always kept me wondering. At any rate, Mark got rid of his appendix and we made it through that time of testing. I thank God we had our precious Savior to go to for wisdom and strength during that trying time.

Following the sickness with the kids, Steve and I had our turn in the hospital as well. I developed an ovarian cyst that required surgery and a three-day hospitalization. Steve had amoebic dysentery, which required a day of IV antibiotics in the hospital and a very long time recovering. I later got amoebic dysentery also but fortunately didn't have to be hospitalized. We had several other dysenteries during those four years but fortunately escaped some of the other tropical diseases such as malaria and dengue fever which are brought on by infected mosquitoes. Eye infections were also very common, and often caused blindness. Blind beggars were everywhere! Mark had a severe eye infection when he was about four years old in Lucena. We thank God it was only in one eye and no one else in the family got it. God was again watching over us. This was particularly common in the rural areas.

The tropics have the usual pests like flies, cockroaches, crickets, rats and termites. In Lucena we had rats that chewed on my Tupperware. In Makati the termites chewed up my flannelgraph lessons and other teaching materials. Cockroaches got into our closets and cupboards, eating holes in clothing and destroying food. Mold would accumulate on our shoes in damp weather. We learned to get used to some of the problems and frustrations but most difficult were the illnesses that struck our children. Through it all, our children never resented being missionary kids for which we are so grateful. They still love to reminisce about life in the Philippines.

# Chapter 30

## *Traffic Accidents*

Accidents are also common occurrences in the Philippines. Many Americans will not drive in Manila traffic. Even our military friends from Clark Air Base sought to avoid driving in Manila. The highways looked similar to a large parking lot at times appearing to have no definite lanes. Cars, busses, jeepneys, and trucks were sitting at various angles. Traffic, at times, didn't move very fast, so it was easy to just follow the car in front of you and then realize you had gone past your destination. The traffic laws were not followed as they should be, consequently accidents happened quite often and speed limits were not carefully heeded.

One night Steve had gone to a Bible study in a home in Makati. I was home with the kids when a telephone call came from one of the men who was with Steve in the Bible study. He spoke very slowly and softly saying, "Mum, Pastor met an accident." At the sound of his sad voice, my heart started pounding as he described the location, which way Steve was driving and where the other car was coming from and all the details. I was getting weak and feeling faint when he finally said, "But he's okay." Whew, what a relief! The car, however, was not okay. They towed it away to be repaired, which literally took months due to ordering some of the parts from the

States as well as very slow workmen. We were back to taking taxis, jeepneys, or busses for a long time.

Fortunately, Bob Skivington had an extra vehicle loaned to him for some reason, and he was willing for us to use it until our car was repaired. However, it was an old milk truck presumably from the United States. There were no doors on either side so one had to be careful and anchor oneself well while riding. We will never forget this vehicle for two reasons. First, our Japanese neighbors provided us with two tickets for box seats to the Tokyo Symphony at the fancy Cultural Center in downtown Manila. This required that I wear a long dress and Steve be dressed in his best. How could we bypass such an opportunity? We hoped no one would see us as we got in or out of the milk truck. It was an exciting concert with a break at intermission where we were privileged to meet some visiting ambassadors. One commented that we didn't look like missionaries. If he had seen our mode of transportation, he may have retracted that statement. We had a good laugh all the way home and were thankful for this strange mode of transportation.

At one point in the evening a spray of flowers was presented to someone in the balcony and accidently fell to the lower floor level. Of all things, it landed on the head of Imelda Marcos. It was obvious that people tried to keep their dignity but we heard a lot of of snickering.

The second reason we wouldn't forget that milk truck, was an occasion when Steve drove it to a youth meeting with our youth loaded inside. Our Terri piled into the back with the rest of the group where they couldn't see out and Tami sat next to Steve in the front. On the way back to Makati on the super highway, the steering mechanism went out. Steve did his best to maneuver the truck, however, it ended up at the side of the road on its side. Steve extended his foot to try to keep the vehicle erect but it fell on his foot resulting in a break and a long time on crutches. Tami had a severely sprained ankle but to my knowledge, none of the other youth were injured. In explaining the scene Steve said it looked like a white elephant lying on its side on the edge of the road. Again we were thankful it was not worse but we were taking public transportation for quite some time before the car was repaired. This was most difficult for Steve due to the crutches he had to put up with.

With our good friends, Bob and Marge Skivington

Yes, there are many calamities in life but we found God has some purpose in them all. In studying His Word, we read of many of God's servants who suffered greatly. Others in the historical records of war, famine and pestilence have suffered more than we have. God gave us great peace no matter what He brought upon us because He gave us His comfort and hope in all things.

Back on the home front, there were hardships and happy times. Steve's mom had open-heart surgery to have a left mitral valve replaced. We waited a long time to hear how it went but eventually heard she was doing well. It was a rough surgery, however, as she was unable to have much, if any anesthesia. I know she was aware of what was going on through the entire process.

Exciting news came as Hildi wrote that dear Aunt Hazel who had been like a second mom to my family was getting married at the age of sixty to her first cousin, Walter Olson. Walter had lost his wife who had a bad heart. Aunt Hazel had been a bridesmaid or maid of honor at his first wedding. Now she was going to be his bride. They had always been close as cousins and even had the same birthday though she was a little older. We were so happy for them. They were married in the same church Steve and I were married in and it had meaning for her as well because of her dad and brother building the church and pulpit furniture many years before.

Aunt Hazel and Uncle Walter

More good news was that my brother, Ken and wife, Loma had their first son, Kevin Lloyd. We were getting anxious to see these dear ones and meet this little blond, curly headed boy.

Through all that God brought us through, we have had His promises such as this one: "The Lord will keep you from all harm—he will watch over your life; the Lord will watch over your coming and going both now and forevermore" (Psalm 121:7,8 NIV). How we praise Him.

# Chapter 31

## *Baguio Revisited*

Vacation trips to Baguio continued each year and gave us a multitude of memories. I recall our anticipation as we drove the many miles to the mile-high city. On one such occasion, we came to the realization that while we were driving up the mountain, gazing at the moon, our astronauts were surveying the moon with the anticipation of one day landing upon it.

Along with the happiness of getting away to the mountains for relaxation, there always seemed to be some foreboding about the possibility of some untoward incident. Often we were still taking medicine for a parasite and I recall the nausea setting in and having to stop for a "swig" of paregoric, that horrible tasting medicine which kept the diarrhea away. We hoped we could completely recover with some time of rest. Such was the case one time when Steve was recovering from something. He went to bed earlier than I after the long drive to Baguio. While I was still up, I saw him coming down the hall to the bathroom and then heard a crash as if something fell in the bathroom. Lo and behold, he had fainted, falling against the flusher handle of the stool and cutting his nose. I called our fellow missionaries who were upstairs and together we got in touch with a doctor. It seemed it was just his low blood pressure and in his sleepiness I had scared him as he came down the hall. He thought I was in bed and wondered who had broken into the house. That shows what happens to weak bodies in times of stress.

A lady from Switzerland was in charge of the key for the vacation house. Her home was just up the mountain a ways and we enjoyed the walk to her house amid the pine trees and the beautiful view. My imagination transported me briefly to what I thought the Swiss Alps would be like. We sat and visited with this woman and her friendly black Lab. She didn't speak English well but her hospitality was great. When Tami, Terri, and I went there one day she served us tea and cookies. I had never eaten a cookie that contained cheese so was very happy to have the tea which accompanied it. I wonder if it was Swiss cheese. At any rate, we had a unique experience.

Most of our vacations in Baguio were during the Christmas season; however, we did have one where we were assigned by the mission to go up there to work in the house, repainting the inside, making new curtains etc. We thought it was improved, however, not all of our missionaries had the same taste and promptly changed the curtains to something I thought was dreary. We realized how different each of us is and we tried to keep peace within the missionary family.

Some things in the city of Baguio were very old fashioned such as a grocery store where the customer's change would come from a basket attached to a cable from the upper level of the store. It took me back in time to the old country stores in America. Our kids enjoyed the novelty as we relished the nostalgia.

While in the States, Steve and I both enjoyed the coconut topped hostess cupcakes. There was one bakery in Baguio that made them but left out the cake part on the bottom. Though incomplete, they were tasty and we very much enjoyed other goodies such as cinnamon crisps from that bakery.

Several times our friend, Vera Ewoldt, who had been Tami's fourth grade teacher, came with us to Baguio. She was a part of our church and became a dear friend. The most memorable part of that vacation was the rain that poured down for almost 30 days straight, absolutely no let up at all. It was a hard rain and blurred our vision even to the house next door. We simply had to go out to the market whether we wanted to or not. We donned our tennis shoes, as we waded in water that completely covered our shoes. We had to think of activities we could do indoors such as sewing, putting puzzles together, and playing games. Vera was great at entertaining the kids in ways never thought of before. We had difficulty doing laundry, as we couldn't get the clothes dry. We strung clothes on a line near the fireplace but often the rain came down the chimney and put the fire out.

We could not leave Baguio due to landslides and floods. Our time kept being extended. Phone calls were made to Manila. No transportation was moving. It was time for school to start at Faith Academy. Vera was supposed to be there to teach and our kids were to be in school. There was nothing we could do. Other missionaries we knew were all in the same predicament. None of us could move. It was rather strange but we happened to be reading about Noah and the flood for our family devotions at the time. We began to wonder if we were going to experience forty days and forty nights of this torrential rain. We didn't see the sun until the twenty-eighth or twenty-ninth day when the sun peeked out just briefly. It was a sign that soon things would change for the better.

When we were finally able to leave, we had to drive through what had become like a river and Steve had to keep the gas peddle down so water would not get in the tail pipe. We made it across but the tail pipe on the car had fallen off and he had to take off his belt to fasten it on until we could get it properly fixed. Upon arriving home, we noticed all of our shoes in the closet were mildewed having been closed up all that time. Manila had gotten its share of bad weather too but we were thankful to be home.

Vera was with us another time in Baguio when she and I decided to take the kids to the open market. The twins were close to ten and Mark was six years old at the time. To get an idea what the market was like, I will let Mark tell you his side of the story as he later wrote it.

This is just a portion of his story he entitled: *"Lost in an Uncommon Market."*

*The open Market was a conglomeration of shops jumbled together ranging from butcher shops to tourist traps. It was interesting to go there and bargain with the shopkeepers. My dad enjoyed that the most out of all of us I think. Especially interesting to me were the natives. The men looked like Elena's husband (caretakers at our Baguio house) with bare, muscular legs transported by sinewy duck-like feet. The women were short, squatty stumps who were nearly, and oftentimes stronger than the men. Some wore tribal skirts with psycedelic blouses or different colored sweaters that rarely matched. On their heads many wore snake-bone headbands while others wore various strange headgear. Others carried pots perfectly balanced atop their heads and on their ears many had astounding earrings that stretched the earlobes considerably out of shape. Ornaments adorned the noses of others but the craziest thing I found was the way the old women squatted in the aisles smoking long, narrow cigars with the lighted ends in their mouths!*

*My Mom, my sisters, Miss Ewoldt, and I arrived there*

*in early afternoon. The sky was overcast and looked as if it might rain. My father, being tired from the trip, stayed home and rested. We walked up and down a few aisles when I came upon a shop selling toys. My mom bought me a toy machine gun. I was intrigued by the little trucks and cars only for a moment but when I turned around my mother and sisters were gone! I was left alone with my toy gun in my hand amidst a swarm of short, dark-haired, brown-skinned natives. I frantically walked up the aisle which actually was a road and came to the butcher shop. The red, bloody flesh was hanging in the open air with flies congregating all around. I then heard the squeal of a butchered pig and desperately headed back the opposite way. Everything seemed in chaos. These strange people were going every which-way but seemed oblivious to me. I ventured further, machine gun in my hand, till I came to a dark alley crowded and pulsating with native life. At the entrance sat an old shriveled woman with a dried apple face. She emitted a garbled utterance to me in her native tongue and motioned for me to come over to her. If the sight of her wasn't enough, this was! I bolted back in the direction I came, nearly panicking. With little hope, I decided to pray. I leaned up against a stall and closed my eyes "Dear Lord, please help me find Mom. I don't know where she is."*

*A Filipino man glared down at me with a strange look just as I decided to go back to the car. Halfway there, like a tall lighthouse, beaming over a troubled sea, I saw Miss Ewoldt. My fears quickly drained from my body as relief surged into its place. Her uncommon stature in this uncommon place assured me of my safety.*

*"Do you know where my mom is?"*

*"No, but I think she may be in here buying vegetables."* *Sure enough there she was with my sisters, checking out the cauliflower.*

Baguio Market

# Chapter 32

## God Never Forgets

Several years had passed since I had asked the Lord to help me find a book that might be a blessing to my Chinese friend in Baguio. I asked that I might find a book about a Chinese Christian who had lived in the pre-communist era. I never forgot my friend and visited her many times when we vacationed in Baguio. She was always friendly and usually invited us into her apartment at the back of her shop. Always she served us tea and some little treat. We discussed the many beautiful things in her home that came from old China. On one occasion she played a classic piano piece for us. We discussed differences in Christianity and Buddhism, emphasizing that we had a living God, a Savior who had died for us and rose again and was presently living to intercede for us. We know at one time she believed this back in Shanghai where she played the piano in a Baptist Church.

While in Baguio our last time, we were browsing in the OMF (Overseas Missionary Fellowship) bookstore. I began to check out the books on sale at a table at the front of the store. Suddenly I noticed a book that had an oriental looking cover entitled, "Queen of the Dark Chamber." I glanced at the back cover and read the first few lines which stated, "This remarkable autobiography gives an inside picture of the China that has gone. It reveals the Lord's working in winning one life to Himself and using that life, even through suffering to win scores to Himself." We were in a rush that day but I felt quite safe in purchasing this book. I purchased two of them so I could read it myself in order to interact with her if possible. After returning to our vacation house, I continued reading the back cover: "Intellectual, educated, the daughter of a high Chinese official, Miss Tsai shares the story of her conversion and of God's sustaining grace in a unique witness to the power of God. Over 100,000 copies have been published in thirty-eight printings of the American editions. In addition, *Queen of the Dark Chamber* has been published in Britain and in numerous foreign languages including Chinese, Korean, Japanese, German, Norwegian, Spanish, Thai, Italian, Finish and three languages of India. Editions are in preparation in French, Dutch, Tibetan and Russian."

Concerning this book, Billy Graham wrote: "The author has made us feel the heartbeat of a nation and has done much to interpret the sufficiency of Christ to a great and needy people. In her furnace of affliction Miss Tsai has discovered the secret of spiritual refining. In her dark chamber of infirmity she has found the Light of the World." I knew at this point God must have led me to this book and decided since it was the Christmas season, this would be my gift to my friend. I gift-wrapped it and presented it to her a few days later. She happily accepted it but did not open it. I'm not sure if she was following Chinese or Philippine culture but I do know Filipinos do not usually open gifts in the presence of the giver, so I was not surprised.

Before leaving Baguio for Manila, I stopped by the gift shop to bid farewell to my friend. We chatted a bit and then she said, "Oh, thank you for the book. I know this lady. I was the one who bought all of her things." Since

I hadn't read the book as yet, I wasn't sure exactly what that meant. However, I was amazed that God led me to a book written by someone with whom my friend was personally acquainted. After returning home, I was eager to delve into the amazing book and found that Christiana Tsai was born into a family of distinction, her father was governor general during the late Manchu dynasty of the province of Kiang-su. She lived in a palatial home with great riches and many servants. It was a large family of eighteen children, therefore, when Christiana was born, they gave her a name that meant "too many." However, within the family she was simply called "Sister Seven" as most girls in the Orient at that time had no first name. They simply designated the children by their birth order. It was only later that this dear girl came to know Christ and chose the name "Christiana."

Bedridden for twenty-three years due to a crippling disease, this young woman, with God's undergirding strength, accomplished more for God than many a person that is healthy and whole. She had a rare form of malignant malaria in her bone marrow. She could not tolerate light as it caused severe pain in her eyes. The disease involved many other parts of her body as well. She felt like her body was burning in spite of a very cold room. Severe nausea made it difficult to retain food. Her mouth was sore, her hands were black, and knuckles cracked open to the bone. Though her room was as dark as they could make it, she had to wear very dark glasses. At times God would revive her out of her suffering, then a relapse would follow.

Mary Leaman, a missionary with the China Inland Mission, had a great influence on Christiana and became her primary teacher, caregiver and co-worker. Together they prepared the translations of the Scriptures into phonetic script. This made it possible even for the poorly educated to learn to read the Bible. This task took many years and was accomplished through two women who were very ill. They worked together giving their lives for the work of God in China.

Communism then entered China and Mary Leaman was put in a prison camp for her faith. Christiana sent her servants to bring Mary food and whatever supplies she could get. Then it was that Christiana sold all of her lovely belongings in order to see Mary Leaman freed from prison camp. They soon had to leave China even though they were both too ill to travel. Christiana desperately needed a very rare medication and a surgery on her hands before she could think of traveling but God undertook as these two saints of God literally held each other up as they embarked on their ocean voyage to America.

This is not the end of the story of Christiana Tsai as she wrote another book entitled simply, *Christiana Tsai,* as miracles continued here in the U.S.A. I highly recommend you read both books on her amazing life, published by Moody Press.

Wow! It was almost unbelievable that God would not only lead me to a book about someone my friend knew personally but who would have ever dreamed that those lovely works of art I had many times admired in her home were previously owned by Christiana Tsai.

It was a great sacrifice to give them up, but those things no longer mattered to Christiana. I don't see how my friend could keep from finding her way back to God after reading about His amazing work in this servant of God back in the China she loved.

I didn't realize I would never see my friend again. I had fully hoped to follow-up with her in future years. Steve did get back to Baguio years later when visiting the Philippines. He took the second book, *Christiana Tsai,* in hopes of giving it to our friend, however, the Chinese gift shop was gone and so was she. I have peace, however, in knowing that God was in my encounter with this woman because of that very special answer to prayer. It served to grow my faith in Him "being confident of this very thing, that He who has begun a good work in you will complete it until the day of Jesus Christ" (Philippians 1:6).

Not only has my faith grown because of God's special answer to my prayer, I have sensed God's love for me in leading me to exactly what I asked from Him resulting in a greater love and closeness to Him. I'm sure He knew I would also need the encouragement from the life of Christiana Tsai. I have never known of a woman so ill that God has used so mightily and it has helped me go on in spite of my times of affliction in my later years. God is always faithful to those who put their trust in Him. At times Christiana said she would not be able to finish her second book for she was simply too weak and ill. Friends around her told her she must press on, as people needed her story.

I began this book due to the prompting of the Holy Spirit and friends and relatives. However, the task just seemed too overwhelming and I kept putting if off. I also felt so unworthy to share my life with anyone. I had lived with so much shame in my younger years. Then I became ill where I could not often leave my home due to an autoimmune disease. I wasn't bedridden but had a definite problem. Somehow I needed to find a way to serve the Lord in my home. I prayed and asked God how I could serve Him if I couldn't go to Bible studies at church and other things I always participated in. Since I began this book, I have been hospitalized several times, had a heart ablation and dealt with this disease for over twenty years. Hardly a day goes by without some problem in my digestive system and I have often feared I could not finish writing this book. Then I remember Christiana whose illness was far more serious and God seems to say, He will faithfully see me through so "I press toward the goal for the prize of the upward call of God in Christ Jesus" (Philippians 3:14).

# Chapter 33

## *Trophies of Grace*

We were continually amazed at how God worked in our ministry in Makati. There were two families that were leaders from the beginning of our time there, the Chanco family and the Bautista family.

Tony and Yasu Bautista were in the Capitol City Baptist Church where we attended during our language school days. They were now living in the Makati area where he worked for the Loyola Life Plan. Rueben Chanco also worked with him. We found out that my husband Steve had led Rueben to Christ in those earlier days at Capitol City Baptist Church after an evangelistic meeting. Now these two were stalwarts in the church in Makati. Tony's wife Yasu was Japanese and they had two daughters, Mimi, and Sakurako. Later God gave them a son, Joshua. Today they are of course grown and married and serving the Lord. Mimi, the eldest is married to a Philippine sculptor and living in Japan, Sakurako is also married and I believe she is living in Canada. Josh, the youngest has been a pastor in a couple churches in Japan but is now pastoring in Canada. Josh keeps us up to date with the family on Facebook.

The Bautista family

Reuben Chanco was married to Chari, a vibrant little woman who loved the Lord deeply and was a real witness to all she knew. She was responsible for bringing many to the Lord. Together, they raised their children to serve the Lord and are faithful to this day. All are active in the Lord's work. The oldest daughter, Rowena, is married to a thriving pastor and Roxanne, another daughter is a Christian school teacher. Rene Chanco has earned a doctor's degree at Western Seminary in Portland, Oregon. He and his wife are missionaries in the Philippines where he serves in leadership and teaching at Asian Theological Seminary. It was a thrill recently to see on Facebook, a picture of him on CNN news in the Philippines where he was speaking about some national issue. Ron, another son, has also become a pastor. Both Reuben and Chari are now with the Lord but were found faithful to the end. Their children began serving the Lord in their local high schools and are carrying on the legacy of their parents to this day. We hear from several of them on Facebook with evidence of their continued service and hearts for God. That goes for many of the provincial young people as well. How wonderful it is to keep in touch with them across the miles.

The Chanco family

Chari had a friend that owned a restaurant and brought her to church where she accepted the Lord. This woman immediately became convicted about serving alcoholic beverages in her restaurant and one day decided she would no longer do so. Everyone warned her that she would lose business. However, God blessed her and she actually had an increase in her business.

Another family who provided leadership in our church was General Sam Sarmiento and his family. Sam was one of the few Filipinos who had actually grown up in a Christian home. It was a joy to meet his parents one day in their home in Baguio. They were a musical family and we had a short time of singing together around their piano. They only had two sons, Sam and his brother, Eliezer was a physician married to a medical doctor who was educated in the United States. Ellie, as he was called, was also gifted in music. He played the organ and often directed the citywide Messiah concerts at Christmas time. He also took medical teams up in the tribal areas now and then to minister to those who needed medical care. General Sarmiento was chairman of our deacon board and a very honorable man. We all remember so well when he arrived in a helicopter at our Sunday School picnic held in an outlying area. He was the number one general in the Philippine Air Force under President Marcos. Frances, his wife, was a nurse and very active in the women's ministry and the choir. Their four children, John, James, Peter, and Ailene also were a vital part of the ministry there in Makati.

The Sarmiento family

It was our privilege to get to know a man named Alfonso Noa. He and all of his family came to know the Lord. Mr. Noa built stereo systems and was very good with electronics. He had an interesting history, that of fighting for the USAFE (United States Army in the Far East) during World War II. He was a survivor of the Bataan Death March and recalled the horrors of being placed in a building with a large company of soldiers where there was standing room only and not much moving air. People were sick with dysentery, enduring vomiting and diarrhea while they endured the heat and humidity. He remembers being near a crack in the wall where he was able to get a bit of air.

Mr. Noa always tried to make the best of every situation and he decided to make a musical instrument he could play as they marched toward Bataan. He called it his "sardinarias," a sort of guitar made from an oval shaped U.S. sardine can. He used telephone wires for the strings, had a pick made from a phonograph record, and used a small medicine bottle to slide on the fret area, (however, there were no frets) to change the pitch. It was played similarly to a dulcimer. He made beautiful music on this instrument and played for a UFO talent contest, and won the grand prize. We were privileged to have him visit us in the States years later where he played for our college chapel as well as at Palmcroft Baptist Church in Phoenix where he received a standing ovation. He made a similar guitar for our son Mark which he still has. The only difference was he couldn't find the bigger U.S. oval sardine can so he had to use a smaller one.

Mr. Noa saw to it that all of his family came to Christ. His wife was skeptical for a while but soon she was faithful along with him. They had one problem though. They had a difficult time getting rid of their idols, which were images of the virgin Mary and other saints. In the

Philippines, images like this are somewhat of a status symbol and they have heard over and over again that if they got rid of these idols, bad luck would befall them. Consequently they hung unto them as they were also considered valuable.

One night they were to have Bible study at their home and the pastor who followed us came to the home and he wondered why the one daughter-in-law who had normally been a part of the study was not there. They told him she was upstairs and not feeling well. The pastor went to check on her and found she was not acting in her right mind. The pastor then told them if they wanted her to get well, they must get rid of their idols. Finally the Noa's realized they must fully follow God and began to destroy the idols. Mr. Noa couldn't help but notice the helplessness of the idols as they fell to the floor and cracked into many pieces rolling hither and yon. A little later the daughter-in- law came down from upstairs and spoke to the pastor saying, "Oh, Pastor, I didn't know you were here." Now, however, she was in her right mind. Oh, the power of God that is released when one obeys!

Mr. Noa had a good friend who was a doctor. This doctor had other male friends who met periodically in a sort of clubhouse. These men had told Mr. Noa that if he got rid of his idols bad luck would befall him. Interestingly God had another plan. Right after they had destroyed the idols, Mr. Noa got a letter from a lawyer in the United States saying he had been looking over his records and found that Mr. Noa was owed a pension from the U.S. army for his time of service during the war. That was a real testimony to these men. Mr. Noa then invited Steve to come to their clubhouse to speak to them. The doctor accepted Christ as his Savior at that time.

Mr. and Mrs. Noa with some of their family

Another story of great interest and blessing is the story and testimony of a wealthy, attractive woman who lived in the most prestigious part of Makati. Her family was involved in several large businesses and her husband and his family were well known in governmental affairs. This family had been a contact of the missionary who preceded us. Steve went to visit them at their home and expected to be greeted at the door by a servant. Instead, this lovely Filipino couple met him there and invited him to come in. This opened the door to a wonderful friendship and eventual faith in Christ. Steve learned later that the husband asked his wife, "how much did he ask for?" They, being well to do, were continually pressed by various religious organizations for contributions. She told her husband, "He didn't ask for anything." After this Steve would visit them about once a month and every time have opportunity to explain the Bible and the way of salvation to the wife.

Finally on one occasion, the wife asked, "Reverend,

you've been explaining a lot of stuff to me but what is it you are really driving at?" Steve had tried over and over to get her to see that one has to pray and by faith ask Jesus to come into one's heart and life to receive salvation. On this occasion he said, "You need to pray and ask Jesus to save you." He said she could make this decision right then and there in their living room. She agreed and began to pray asking Jesus to come into her life, forgive her sins and to save her. She told Steve sometime later that while she was about half way through her acceptance prayer she'd said to herself, "I mean this prayer." It became very obvious that truly the Holy Spirit had prompted her real decision, for her life gave immediate evidence of the new birth in Jesus.

Steve began follow up but she was not ready to step out and become part of our church family. In fact she became more ardent in her Roman Catholic faith but all the time reading the Bible and telling people what Christ meant to her now.

She bought a huge case of Bibles and went to a nearby Catholic high school and handed out Bibles to the students. They dubbed her, "Woman of the Bible." In addition to this, she helped raise money to build two Roman Catholic churches. She would get artists to paint pictures and donate their works to an art auction held at her home. The proceeds then were donated to the erection of these Catholic Churches.

It is important in evangelism to realize that sometimes you have to work with great patience before you see the convert take their stand for Jesus in a clear and unambiguous way. This pattern continued in this manner with this woman for another year and all this time she was growing in the Lord but was fearful to leave her former Catholic faith.

However, one evening Steve was at their home and

the wife said to him, "Reverend, you've been coming here for a long time" and Steve was fearful she would say, "and I think it is time for you to stop coming." Instead she said, "Would you pray that I will make it to your church tomorrow?" Of course we would pray and sure enough she came and joined right in the adult Sunday School lesson. Her children, maids and driver all came as well. We were thrilled. After Sunday school, however, she said she had to hurriedly leave and get to her own church. She kept up this pattern for a year. The Bible studies continued in their home and one day she said, "Reverend, I notice that the Bible says, once you accept Christ as your Savior, you need to be baptized, so when can I be baptized?" Steve then had to go over the true meaning of baptism and gave her the knowledge that Christ was sacrificed once for our sins and there was no need for him to be re-sacrificed through some ritual of our own doing. She began to see the difference and was ready to be baptized.

Arrangements were made for the service in one of our associated churches that had a baptistery. Others were baptized that night as well as our son, Mark, at the age of eight. Typical of a boy his age, he saw no need to be quietly led into the water but jumped in as if he was in a swimming pool. He wasn't trying to be funny but just did what a boy of his age would do. To us it sort of took away from the solemn occasion but this was a very meaningful time for this woman and her family.

Following our friend's baptism, the Bible studies continued weekly in her home. She was so anxious for others in her family to come to know Christ. Then one day she was asked to give a testimony on behalf of her sister who was seeking an annulment for her marriage due to a very serious situation in which her sister's life was endangered.

To do this, our friend had to meet with an annulment judge. He had a PHD in canon law from the Gregorian Institute in Rome and was also working on a PHD in education. One of the first questions this judge asked was, "What is your religion?" She said, "Well, Father, I was a Roman Catholic, but I am a Baptist now." Immediately he asked, "What made you change?" She gave him her testimony and also said, "By the way, Father, we have Bible study every Thursday night with Rev. Sonmor." He then asked, "Can I come?" She of course invited him and told Steve he would be having dinner with a priest the next week. Needless to say, it put pressure on Steve and he felt he really had to prepare for this.

By the time next Thursday came around, God seemed to tell Steve he should simply give what he was planning to give before he knew a priest was coming. Very likely he just needs to hear the truth of God's Word. During the Bible Study discussion, our friend approached the priest with, "Father, how can we know we are going to get to heaven?" He replied, "Well, God is not a computer God. He doesn't keep track of everything. Just do the best you can and you'll make it." She replied, "Come on Father, I tried that for years and it doesn't work." She proceeded to share with him again. He then had tears in his eyes and said, "Pray for me, I have lost my faith."

The priest then asked if there were any other services he could come to and Steve informed him of our Sunday School and church services and he did come. He dressed in ordinary clothes so that no one knew he was a priest. He kept coming until his superior told him he had been going out too much. We had to leave on furlough but when we got back on July 4, 1975, this judge left the priesthood and he said, "All of my companions wished me God's speed."

This priest was Chinese and listened to a Chinese

broadcast from the Far East Broadcasting Company, on DZAS, the Manila station. He happened to get well acquainted with the Chinese woman who spoke the messages and through her he made a decision to accept Christ as his Savior. He later married this Chinese woman and the last we heard he went on to Asian Theological Seminary preparing to minister to the Chinese people.

These experiences illustrate so well the thought from an old chorus, "You tell the one next to you and I'll tell the one next to me," and together we will reap the joys that God has planned for us to enjoy in the heavenlies when the crowns we receive can be laid at the feet of Jesus to praise Him for all that He has done. How blessed we are to be a part of His forever family! To God be the glory!

A home Bible study in Makati

# Chapter 34

## Second Furlough

It was now March 30, 1974, and our time in Makati was winding down. We moved out of our house of many wonderful memories and moved to our mission guesthouse until school was out for the year, which was on April sixth. After a few days of field conference where we had our pre-furlough interview, we found ourselves at the Manila Airport in the VIP room which General Sarmiento had secured to bid goodbye to the many friends who came to see us off for our homeland. We were presented with sampaguita leis (the national flower of the Philippines) and were soon aboard the plane where we were seated next to our friends, the Lyons. We had a brief stop in Okinawa and then flew on to Tokyo where Marty and Arlene Shaw, our Japan missionaries, met us for a brief visit bringing a gift for each of us. Soon we were on an all-night journey to Honolulu, Hawaii where we were to minister in a missions conference at International Baptist Church and Bible College for the next week.

As we arrived at the Honolulu airport, I was taken by surprise as a young man presented me with a lei and a kiss on the check and Steve also received the same from a young lady. We learned this was the custom in Hawaii. Dr. Jim Cook was the pastor of the church and President of the Bible College and had formerly served with our mission in India, Ceylon, and the Philippines. His parents, Dr. Bill and Jenny Cook, were also a part of the ministry there and we knew of their great work in India where Jim grew up. They were all from Minnesota so had ministered often in our own churches there. Actually Jim had been Steve's counselor in Camp Chetek in Wisconsin and remembered him well because when Steve's billfold was stolen and he had no money for treats, Jim saw to it that he had a replacement for what he lost. To a young boy, that was something he never forgot. Now he had the privilege to minister in his church.

One of the first events we enjoyed was an Easter Sunrise Service like none we'd ever seen before. About a thousand people gathered near an ocean cove and worshiped with trumpets and other musical instruments and singing as the sunrise took place. What an awesome privilege we had to be in such a thrilling location. The church too was beautifully decorated with an abundance of flowers not only in the front of the church but hanging from the ceiling in large arrangements. I particularly remember the Easter lilies entwined in the punctured copper cross at the front of the church.

We stayed with a dear family for the week and were treated so wonderfully. Each evening, after a lovely meal in various homes we ministered at the church in music and speaking. One night the children joined with us in singing. The Frank family was one we especially remembered as Tami and Terri enjoyed playing with their daughter, Beth, not knowing that one day she would be in college with them. Beth eventually married Eric Yodis, one of my music students and are missionaries in Ukraine.

That week brought many blessings, one of which was a boost to our support and another was seeing the Bible college supply the funds to purchase a car for Philippine evangelist, Paul Mortiz. We of course enjoyed the beautiful scenery of the islands, a few shopping trips, and making many new friends.

Our arrival in Hawaii

On April 20, 1974, we flew to San Jose, California where Larry Chappell was the pastor of a Baptist Church. Steve led Larry to Christ back in college days when he did camp work in Colorado. The people of the church met us holding a huge banner saying, "Thank You for leading our Pastor to Christ." They presented gifts to each of us, got us settled in a lovely motel and then brought us to the pastor's home for a meal and a time of fellowship. The next day we were able to serve in the church and once again visit in the pastor's home in the evening. Missionary life had provided much excitement that we never anticipated. God never shortchanges His servants.

Once again we landed in Seattle where we were met by Uncle Wes, Aunt Lil and cousin Karen. Wes again bought something for the kids and then took us to the Farrell's Ice Cream Parlor that was so popular at that time. We got to bed quite late and knew the day ahead was going to be a busy one.

Grandpa Sonmor had nine sisters, three of whom lived

in the Seattle area. Aunt Gene and husband, Ray Urness lived in Poulsbo, which necessitated taking a ferry to see them. Later we visited Aunt Evelyn Vokalek and son Bill followed by another trip by ferry to Aunt Jo and Ed Swenson's home where we had a lovely meal. I remember especially the fresh asparagus from her garden. It is one of my favorite vegetables and it wasn't available in the Philippines. This happened to be Grandpa Sonmor's birthday so he was blessed with a phone call from all three sisters and our family as well. We finished our time in Seattle with more relatives at Wes and Lil's home followed by a good night of rest.

Prior to leaving in the morning we saw cousin Kristi and her new husband and Karen and Lil took us to the airport. We were all pretty keyed up as we got on the Northwest flight to Minneapolis as we greatly anticipated seeing all of our immediate family again. They had made arrangements for all of us to have a nice meal at the Viking Restaurant in Minneapolis. Steve's folks were going to drive back to Wisconsin to the farm that night and Mark eagerly wanted to go with them. The rest of the family all came to our house where Charlotte and Phoebe had brought a cake so we had a further time of fellowship. Charlotte and Phoebe had added some lovely decorative touches to our house as well as to the farmhouse. The farm kitchen was enlarged with new cupboards and the rest of the house redecorated. It looked like a lovely bed and breakfast place, which the family enjoyed for years to come.

It was exciting to see Aunt Hazel so happily married to our "Uncle" Walter and to see Kevin, the new addition in Ken and Loma's family. He was almost three and such a cute, curly-headed blond toddler. I remember a time when he was threatened with a spanking at our house and his answer was, "Auntie Maren doesn't have a paddle stick!" Was this a preview of what was to come in future years? He always had a sense of humor and we praise God he has grown up to be a church worship leader, a great musician, and servant of God.

Our furlough proved to be a very busy time. There were the usual missionary duties, like medical exams, not the least of which was the dreaded one at Mt. Sinai Hospital in Chicago. All returning missionaries had to have the dreaded purge to make sure all of the parasites were gone and I think all would agree that it was the worst tasting stuff they ever swallowed. Immediately upon taking it nausea would set in followed by hours of diarrhea and sometimes vomiting. It was something we endured because we had to. We never knew if it was out of our system enough to even leave the hospital but eventually we would get extremely thirsty due to dehydration. We usually got popsicles for reviving our strength.

Another duty we had was to get new prayer cards done with photos updated. There were interviews at mission headquarters where we discussed the various projects and situations on the field. Then of course it took time to work with our area representatives to arrange the travel schedule for the year. Ours was very extensive and all had to be contacted during that year. For me there was constant correspondence. Oh, what I would have done to have the computers we have today and how much simpler communication would have been if e-mail had been an option!

Steve had at least three trips alone to the Eastern states where he'd be gone for close to a month at a time. He flew the first time and drove the last two times. I still had speaking engagements in the Twin City area, particularly women's meetings, retreats and mother-daughter banquets in Minnesota and Wisconsin. In addition, I served in various capacities at Camp Lebanon in Minnesota.

# Chapter 35

*More Education*

The Conservative Baptist annual meetings were held at Northwestern College that year and Steve was approached about getting a doctor of ministries degree at Western Theological Seminary in Portland. We were excited about it, yet we realized the tremendous amount of work it was going to take. It also meant being in Portland for about a month of classes and then continuing classes in the Twin City area. I knew this would not only be a lot of work for Steve but it would also take much of my time as I would have to type all of the papers and some of these were more like books! We prayed much but it seemed God wanted him to do this so we planned a backpack camping trip to the west, out near Powell, Wyoming and Yellowstone National Park. Charlotte and Phoebe came with us driving their car and us in ours.

After a great time together we had to part ways as Steve drove on to Portland and we headed home over the Big Horn Mountains with his sisters. It was hard to say goodbye but we knew he would be in God's hands and he would be staying with our friends, Bruce and Esther Ker, formerly missionaries in Ceylon and Hong Kong. Bruce had also attended Dallas Seminary prior to our being there and he was now a professor at Western Seminary. God was so good to arrange for Steve to be in their home.

They were so good to him and he enjoyed them so much. God always knows what we need even before we ask.

It was so nice of Charlotte and Phoebe to make this trip with us. As we headed homeward, we drove over the Big Horn Mountains in the evening and had a glorious sight. A shower of rain had refreshed the landscape followed by sunshine which caused the foliage to glisten. It was great to breathe in fragrant, clean air. It seemed every animal around was near the roadside. Cars parked along the highway or moved slowly to view all of the glorious sights. We saw a herd of sheep, a hundred or more, with a shepherd in his covered wagon, then twelve moose, one of which was a baby, eleven elk, thirty-five deer and later a bear. God just seemed to give us a special blessing that night. It kept my mind off from my sadness of leaving Steve who I knew was camping somewhere by himself. We stayed in a lodge in Sheridan, Wyoming that night and the following day drove on through the Dakotas arriving home at 4:00 a.m. very eager to crawl into our beds.

While Steve was in Portland he had the privilege of officiating at Don Good's wedding. Don was originally from Yam Hill, Oregon, a suburb of Portland. He met Ruth Atienza, a Filipina, while he was in the states. Ruth was the daughter of Max Atienza, an evangelist from the Philippines. Don and Ruth went back to the Philippines as missionaries very near Lucena where we first met Don as a Peace Corps worker. They have even gone back to stay during their retirement years still carrying on missionary work. Steve and Don often talk by phone these days and we thank God for this privilege. Don still remembers every word of Steve's testimony.

Steve started his classes on July twenty-second. During the time he was gone, we spent some time in Hastings with Aunt Hazel and Uncle Walter, some time in Princeton, Minnesota with sister Hildi, Bill and Darla, and two of the weeks were spent at Camp Lebanon. Our friend, Vera, also home on furlough doing deputation came to see us a few times and visited the farm with us. We always enjoyed her visits so much.

Steve returned on August 26th and what a happy day that was for all of us. Soon, however, my real work began typing papers and going with Steve to various libraries to look for sources he needed for his remaining courses and papers. We rented an electric typewriter as we didn't have a good one at home. Steve needed illustrations drawn for one of his extensive papers. I believe it was a commentary on the book of John. Brother Ken came to the rescue with his artistic ability and worked many hours, many days and nights to produce those drawings for Steve. It was constant work the rest of our furlough to get all of these papers done, perfected and sent to the seminary.

Before long it was time to register the kids for school, which was to start on September 3rd. Mark was now in third grade at Fair School where the girls had attended before, and Tami and Terri were in seventh grade at Hosterman Junior High in Robbinsdale. Mark got involved in playing basketball and playing trumpet in the beginning band and also joined a little league softball team that he dearly loved. He made many new friends. The girls played their clarinets in the band and had many new friends both at school and at Robbinsdale Baptist. During the summer, they enjoyed the Crystal neighborhood pool very near to our house and made some special friends at Camp Lebanon as well.

Steve had another trip out East in the spring. While he was gone, the kids and I took turns having a terrible flu where our fevers went as high as 104 degrees. It was good we didn't all get sick at once so we sort of took care of each other. I was so thankful that the kids were older now. The girls did a lot of baby-sitting in the neighborhood, which helped them earn a little extra money, and I knew I could trust them to care for Mark as well.

It seemed the furlough year flew by with all we had to do. One day we received a call from our field chairman and others who were involved with our Bible college requesting Steve to consider becoming the director of our Conservative Baptist Bible College. This involved much prayer and many phone calls and correspondence.

As I look over my journals for that year, I cannot believe how we could travel as much as we did and do all of the other things. We know it was only God's strength that kept us going. At the same time He blessed us with such great family gatherings and the beauties of His creation in ways we could never imagine.

I know Steve and I were working on many of his seminary papers until the day we were to head back to the Philippines. Charlotte and Phoebe decided to move into their folk's former house in Minneapolis so we had to rent our house to someone else. Fortunately we were able to rent it to Paul and Mary Pegors, missionaries with CBFMS in Pakistan and brother Ken would be in charge if and when they were to move out. Now everything was pretty well set for us to get back to our work in the Philippines with a new assignment along with continual ministry in Makati.

# Chapter 36

*The Turnaround*

Family gatherings preceded our departure for our third term of missionary service. We flew first to San Francisco where fellow missionaries, Maynard and Shirley Eyestone met us as well as Joe and Florence Leach, our college friends with whom we stayed for a few days. Joe and Florence treated us like royalty taking us to see Muir Woods one day and another evening took us in one of his planes to a restaurant where we had a great dinner. Their oldest daughter took care of our kids and their younger ones. We had never been treated so royally before. A car had been reserved to pick us up at the airport taking us to "The Point" restaurant. The flight home was so beautiful as we observed the lights on the Bay Bridge and the entire bay area.

We made a few last-minute purchases the next day and participated in the mid-week service at the Leach's church in the evening where Steve shared our missionary work and vision for this coming term.

We departed from the San Francisco airport the next day and met the Billings family who were also heading back to Manila on our flight. The plane stopped in Honolulu for about an hour providing Steve enough time to call our friend, Jim Cook, though he couldn't reach him.

Twenty-two hours later we arrived in Tokyo followed by a brief stop in Okinawa and on to Manila. Our kids were so tired; they slept through the entire flight.

About half of the Makati church came to welcome us in Manila. Nong and Annie Curioso, a delightful young couple who had begun coming to the church before our furlough, brought our own car in which we were able to load our luggage. It was good to see how they had grown in the Lord and how God had blessed them. They drove us to their new condominium where we had a time of fellowship.

The next night we met for prayer meeting in one of the member's homes and it was to be a time of welcome on the part of the church. I had gotten very sick and we had to leave early. Upon arriving back at the guesthouse, I spent the night in the bathroom with diarrhea and vomiting which lasted for several days.

Later the mission gave a welcome party at the guesthouse for all of us who were returning from our furloughs. The guesthouse would again be our home until we found a home for this term.

July 6, 1975 was our first day back at the Makati Conservative Baptist Church (MCBC). What a thrill it was to hear the three youngest of the Chanco children sing a song in three-part harmony during our "Family Time." They did so well and we were so proud of them. This family had grown in the Lord greatly and was a steady witness in their jobs and schools. We also had a lovely lunch in the home of our missionaries, David and Patti Jo Yount, which included our friend from Makati and the converted priest. It was so good to see the faithfulness of the Lord in their lives as they were living out their newfound faith. The priest had just decided to follow the Lord and attend Asian Theological Seminary and was finally at peace in his heart. The entire church had a welcome party also at our friend's lovely home a short time later.

Soon it was time to get past the partying and move on to the nitty-gritty details of the work which involved the church and Bible College as well as house hunting, updating our drivers' licenses, and other paperwork.

Eventually we moved into the house formerly occupied by the Eyestone's in an area called "Blue Ridge." It was sort of on the way to Faith Academy so the bus drive was not as long for the kids as it had been from Makati. It was farther from the church but closer to the Bible College than we were before. It was an unusual Philippine home in that it had a basement and a sort of mezzanine floor (between the main floor and the basement) with one room, which Steve used for his study. It was a pretty good-sized room and was set off by itself making it a quiet, good place to work as long as it was air-conditioned. The other rooms were adequate and it had a nice yard with grass front and back. The only problem was that the house was situated in a sunken area, like a trough, so when heavy rains came the water ran into the house from both front and back yards. It tended to make the basement rather useless.

We encountered several problems after moving into our house; neither the refrigerator nor the washer were working well, and we had a long wait to get the gas stove connected. We had to do all of our cooking with one electric pan. Needless to say, it took some creativity for a while to even fix a meal. Eventually we got the stove working but the refrigerator and washer had to be sent out for repair for a few days. In the midst of it all, school was starting so we had to make lunches for the kids and try to have clothes ready for all of us. It was rather difficult without all of our facilities.

Both Steve and I were involved in teaching at

Conservative Baptist Bible College, (CBBC) where he was also the new director. It was a big job to not only prepare courses, but Steve had to meet with faculty and oversee the entire program. I taught music theory and was involved in directing a singing group.

Meanwhile our kids were involved at Faith Academy, Tami and Terri were now freshmen in high school and Mark was in fourth grade. The girls were involved in band, and also played on the girls' basketball team. Tami broke two fingers playing in one of the games so ended up having to be manager of the team, which was somewhat of a disappointment to her. Yes, misfortune seemed to find its way to Tami again but she always took it well and we know God strengthened her because of it. Mark started trumpet lessons, was noticed for his outstanding artistic ability and excelled in all of his classes.

As we began that term of service, Steve and I both got one parasite after another. Steve began to notice he was getting weaker by the day. He found it difficult to go up and down stairs and soon his work began to suffer and others would have to substitute for him. I too kept having nausea and diarrhea, and was also beginning to have other medical issues that I wasn't fully aware of but knew something wasn't right. I had been extremely anemic the year before and had to have iron injections once a month for approximately a year. I spent many days in bed but with the help of medications, we managed to carry on with our responsibilities.

The situation was very troubling to us as we were enjoying our work and having many contacts and responses to the Gospel. I was particularly enjoying the teaching at the Bible College. The sickness carried on for several months and I remember praying, "Lord, please help Steve to get well so we don't have to leave the Philippines." Steve's parents were worried about him and telling him maybe he should come home. We prayed continually about what to do.

One morning I was awakened by these words in my spirit: "Come ye apart and rest awhile" (Mark 6:31KJV). I told Steve about it as nothing like that had ever happened to me before. It was the words that woke me up. We continued to pray. The very next morning I was awakened with the words, "There is a way that seems right to a man but its end thereof is the way of death" (Proverbs 14:12). I thought, *Lord, what can this mean? How does this fit in with our dilemma? Does this mean that it would seem right that we should stay here but that it could mean death?*

It came time for a special banquet for the Bible College. We had invited Jim Cook from Hawaii to be our speaker. He was concerned for Steve as he noticed Steve had some of the signs of illness that his first wife, Sylvia, had prior to her death. He suggested to our missionary chairman that we go to Dr. Link Nelson, an outstanding missionary doctor with ABWE in Malay Balay, Bukidnon Province, on the island of Mindanao. The arrangements were made for us to fly there and be examined by Dr. Nelson. Our friend, Vera Ewoldt with the Free Church Mission had been recently diagnosed with a large number of enlarged lymph nodes and some other issues with her blood, which she couldn't find answers to so she also flew with us to Mindanao. We were grateful for Harold and Darlene Sala with the radio ministry, "Guidelines," who graciously cared for our kids while we were gone. We took a Pal Airlines flight to Cagayan de Oro in Mindanao followed by an S.I.L. (Wycliffe) small plane to Malay Balay. The latter was a beautiful flight as we flew low enough to see the Del Monte pineapples and coconut palms growing together in groves. The islands are truly beautiful and rich in natural resources.

Dr. Nelson gave us thorough examinations and put us through various tests. Between tests, Steve got to watch and assist Dr. Nelson with some surgeries. He thoroughly enjoyed the experience and described Dr. Nelson as an artist with his surgical knife. My problems were primarily dealing with the effects of dysentery for which I could receive medication, but Steve was found to have viral hepatitis that he apparently had for over a year. It was likely caused by amoebic dysentery. Vera was able to cope with her issues with medication also but later found that she had pernicious anemia which would necessitate her to have Vitamin B-12 injections for the rest of her life. Dr. Nelson advised Steve to leave the tropics as soon as possible and remain in the States for at least two years. He was not sure if Steve could ever return to the tropics but would have to be re-evaluated after at least those two years had passed. We heard later on that Dr. Link Nelson was rated as one of the top surgeons in the world, yet here he was spending his life in a far-away place seemingly unknown. God, however, saw his faithfulness and honored him. We were so blessed to be in their home and experience their labors of love. We couldn't have had better care.

Steve was worried that our people would feel as though we had forsaken them if we left the Philippines. He prayed that they would understand. God gave him a verse in Psalms 109:27. "That they may know that this is Your hand, that You, LORD, have done it." We also conferred with Leonard Tuggy, who was now the Overseas Secretary for the Far East with CBFMS. He too, seemed to concur that this was the best decision for now. We would not resign at this point but go home and see what the Lord would do on our behalf. This then was the assurance that God indeed wanted us to leave at that time.

We, of course, had to inform our field chairman, Orman Knight, as well as all of the personnel at the Bible College and the Makati church. Steve's last Sunday was Novemeber 16th. There were lots of tears because of that decision and the church had also gotten word that we had to move out of the auditorium we had rented, by December 13th so to them it seemed everything was falling apart. In spite of this, we had to believe in our hearts, that this is what God had planned. He did supply another place for the church and it continued on.

One day before Steve left we got a paper in the mail, which showed where one of Steve's professors at Western Seminary had left to become president of Southwestern College in Phoenix, Arizona. Steve was surprised, as Don Launstein had been one of his professors for his doctoral studies and he was also a student with us at Dallas Seminary. He showed the paper to me. I hadn't even realized there was a Conservative Baptist Bible college in Phoenix. As Steve read this paper, the Lord seemed to speak to him telling him this is where he would be teaching in the future. I heard him remark, "Hm, I wonder if he needs a missions professor." We thought no more about it and went on with getting Steve packed up to leave on November twenty-third. Missionaries and nationals were there to bid him goodbye.

Meanwhile, our friend, Nong, helped me run errands, and prepare all of our furniture and appliances for sale. We packed books and other personal items in barrels or crates that needed to be shipped to the States. The ensuing days were unbelievably busy and on December 6th we had the big sale that was to start at 5:30 a.m. Some people arrived even earlier and it made it impossible for me to eat the whole day even though there were other folks there to help. I was not feeling well so didn't have much appetite anyway. Vera was there to help me every day and I don't know what I would have done without her.

Soon we moved out of our house and into the guesthouse even though everything wasn't sold. I had to keep going back to the house each day to meet people and try to get everything done. I had another bacillary or something but was able to carry on with nausea and stomach cramps a good share of the time.

Tami and Terri got to play their last basketball game the night before our departure. They were both able to get in at the same time and the team came alive. I was so happy for them. They had spent the night with their friend, Barbie York and Mark had spent the night with the Yount boys. I know it was difficult to leave their Faith Academy friends, yet there was always anticipation to see family as well. I am still amazed at the way the kids responded to these difficult decisions that had to be made. There was never a complaint. They thoroughly enjoyed their lives in the Philippines and God was there for us in every change and transition. Truly, He was our ever-present help in times of trouble.

Mark's birthday was on December 14th, which we celebrated in Manila but at 1:00 a.m. December 15th we left Manila flying first to Tokyo and then to Anchorage, Alaska where it was about thirty-five degrees with light snow falling. Most of the passengers were Filipinos and were not ready for snow and cold weather. It was still December 14th in the States as the Philippines is a day ahead, so Mark got to celebrate his eleventh birthday twice and he thought that was pretty special. From Anchorage, we flew to San Francisco, followed by a flight to Minneapolis. Our family met us and the kids went right to the Wisconsin farm with Grandpa and Grandma Sonmor while Steve and I went to Hastings, Minnesota with Aunt Hazel and Uncle Walter as Steve had an appointment at Mayo Clinic in Rochester, the next day. Tired as I was from the long flight, I got up at 4:00 a.m. the next day to go with Steve for a liver biopsy and other tests. Testing took at least three days in a row of driving to Rochester.

We continued to stay at the farm or with other relatives, as we had to give the Pegors family ample time to find another place to live during their furlough from Pakistan. On January 2, 1976, we were once again able to move into our own house. However, the rat race wasn't ending; in many ways it was just beginning.

The only picture of our third term in Blue Ridge home

Steve leaving for home

# Chapter 37

*Waiting on the Lord*

Steve continued to feel weak throughout most of January and tried to stay away from crowds as much as possible. He had terrible nightmares for a while and due to physical weakness, his nerves were also affected. His report from Mayo Clinic showed that his liver was basically all right but was scarred from the hepatitis. Gradually he began to heal but total healing was still a long way off.

On February 9th we received a phone call from Dr. Don Launstein, President of Southwestern Conservative Baptist Bible College in Phoenix. Steve said afterwards, "I just knew he was going to ask me about teaching missions at the college." Steve told him he would consider it prayerfully. A letter from Dr. Launstein followed a few days later, along with a call from Dr. Warren Webster, General Director of CBFMS. Apparently Dr. Launstein had talked with Dr. Warren Webster, the General Director of CBFMS, about Steve prior to our return to the Philippines but didn't feel he should request Steve to leave his place of service there. However, now that he was home for at least two years, Dr. Webster thought it might be the place for Steve to minister and use his missionary experience.

Because I had previous experience teaching in a Bible college, I told Steve, "Don't tell him I've taught before, because I really need to be home with the kids." He honored my request. Steve then received an application, which he sent in and subsequently was requested to go to meet the college board of directors on April third.

Prior to that date, Steve had to have hernia surgery and was hospitalized for about three days. We also found out that we both had Giardia Lamblia but were told not to take medication till we got a little stronger.

On March 22nd Dr. Launstein called and asked to speak to me. *What in the world does he want to talk to me about? I really don't want to teach.* He said they had been trying to find additional help for their music department and just hadn't been able to find anyone so he just gave up and started going through Steve's file again. He looked at his transcripts and suddenly he said to himself, "I don't think Steve took all of these music courses I see here." Then he looked more closely and saw that it was *my* transcript. When Steve's transcript from Northwestern was sent to them, they had apparently included mine. Therefore, he wondered if I would be able to join the music faculty. This is just what I wasn't looking for but I couldn't help but wonder if God was in this because of the way all of this transpired, so I told him I would be willing to consider a part-time position as long as I could be home when my kids got out of school each day. All of this resulted in my flying to Phoenix with Steve on April 3rd.

We began our meeting in Phoenix at the Launstein's home where we first met with the student council. To our surprise we saw among the students a young man, Vince Trujillo, whom we had just seen in the Mission guesthouse in Manila prior to our departure. He had apparently served as a short-term worker during his summer break. Another surprise was meeting Dr. Ed Simpson, the Academic Dean, who had been chairman of the Bible Department when we were at Northwestern College as students. His wife, Dr. Fran, was chairman of the Christian Education Department here, just as she had been at Northwestern. I had both of them as my teachers and now we were to be on the same faculty. That was a bit intimidating to say the least. Dr. Ed talked to us about our possible course loads and all that was required of us.

A lovely dinner was prepared for us and the members of the college board of directors, after which there was an extensive time of questioning. All of the board members seemed very nice and were favorable to us.

Later, the Simpsons showed us the campus, which was very small at that time. It included an administration building with offices on the main floor and girls' dormitories on the second floor. There was also a good-sized cafeteria, which doubled as a student activity building. Additionally, there was a set of apartments for male students and married students. The library was in a small building that really didn't look like much at all. Nevertheless, we were impressed with the faculty and staff as well as the students.

Southwestern College

The Simpsons also showed us some model homes, a shopping area, their home, and we ate at a cafeteria. We visited further with the Launsteins where we were staying and Steve had to speak at Paradise Valley Baptist Church the next day. We both had bad colds, which made it a bit difficult but God gave strength. Steve had to speak in the evening at Glendale Baptist Church and we got to hear the Southwestern choir that was directed by Mrs. Elaine Hunter, the other member of the music faculty. I was impressed with the way Mrs. Hunter was able to do all she did. Mrs Hunter, a victim of polio, managed to walk slowly with metal crutches but spent most of her time in a wheel chair. In spite of her handicap, she was a very cheerful person. Following the choir concert we went to the Big Apple Restaurant, a popular place in Arizona, for our evening meal.

On April 5th we finally got to see the inside view of the college which housed the offices and classrooms. Steve spoke in the chapel service and we managed to sing a duet in spite of our colds and sore throats. I spent most of the morning talking with Mrs. Hunter about what music courses I would teach and later we talked more with Dr. Simpson and Dr. Launstein about our workloads. A pleasant reprieve came later when Dr. Fran took me shopping where I was able to get a little gift for each of the kids. We flew back to Minneapolis that night mulling over all that we had packed in during those three days. We were told that if our kids attended Southwestern, they would have free tuition. This was a great incentive and we had much to consider and pray about in determining whether or not this was God's will for us.

During the days that followed, Steve was approached by several churches about pastoring and continued to speak in various venues. I too had various speaking engagements including a women's retreat at Northwestern

College for my sister-in-law, Loma's, women's group. I was blessed to have this special time with Loma.

We still had to finish this school year in Minnesota even if we were to go to Phoenix, which gave us some time to pray, prepare and spend quality time with our families. Those were precious days visiting relatives, attending basketball and softball games for Mark and various sporting events for the girls. Mark truly enjoyed his little leagues and school sports and had made many good buddies that he knew he would miss. His team won a tournament and he was thrilled with the individual trophy he received. The girls had their many friends and activities as well. This was truly home for us now and we knew it would be difficult to leave our families again as they had already missed out on so much of our kids' growing up days. Leaving our home that was now fixed up better than ever, and the friendly neighborhood we'd come to love, we kind of felt like nothing was going to be stable again but we came to realize that stability does not mean lack of change but it is moving with God in every circumstance. The Holy Spirit was preparing us to go to Arizona, which we knew now wasn't just a bunch of sand dunes but a beautiful place with mountains and forests that were within a few hours' drive from the desert area. The desert too, had a beauty all its own. Most of all we couldn't get away from the definite call that Steve sensed even before leaving the Philippines and the many circumstances that seemed to confirm that call. That was the case as we headed to the Philippines before and He would be with us again as we moved to Arizona. When we are His, He is always with us.

In view of that, we set to work to prepare our house for sale and had the help of everyone in our family at various times. They were so good to help us paint, lay new carpet, put up wallpaper, do yard work, or help with the cooking.

It provided many opportunities for back yard picnics and get-togethers that we otherwise might not have had. We are thankful for family and friends who were willing to take time from their own routines to do so much for us. They supported us in prayer and other ways while we were in the Philippines and they would continue to do so as we headed into this new venture as well.

# Chapter 38

_____ ~ _____

# Arizona, Here We Come

Our home in Crystal was put up for sale and God blessed us with a buyer almost immediately. A Christian couple, operators of the Christian bookstore near us, was the first to look at it and felt it was just what they needed. It seemed to be an answer to prayer for them as well as for us.

In order to get both cars, a small trailer and a Rider truck to Phoenix, we needed several drivers. Ken and Loma and Grandpa Sonmor all volunteered to help us. What a time we had. We planned to camp out on our journey so this was not an easy adventure. Sidney, our black and white basset hound, was also a part of the entourage.

Our 1961 Falcon, which we purchased new in seminary days, was a bit of a challenge all the way. First it was radiator problems, which occurred twice followed by brake problems. Apparently there was air in the brake line. We put up the tent camping out in Nebraska till we could get the proper help the next day. The campsite was full of gnats that plagued us all night. We were thankful when we could leave that "gnat site" and move on.

Upon leaving Sioux City, Iowa, the top of the radiator on the Falcon came loose. Steve searched for someone to repair it but the man who could do it was out fishing.

Finally in the night he came home and was able to solder the radiator. This forced us to stay overnight, camping out and leaving the next day for New Mexico. In Taos, New Mexico, the generator on the Falcon burned out so we got another generator but were forced again to stay overnight beside the road, south of Taos. The next day we got into Albuquerque, where we were able to get the tire repairs done on the Falcon and Pontiac before starting the final leg of the journey. What else could go wrong?

Somehow we made it from Albuquerque to Phoenix. I was driving the Pontiac with our three kids and was so grateful for Terri who stayed awake with me on that long haul to Phoenix. We arrived at the college at 3:30 a.m. on June 8, 1976, Steve's birthday, to a quiet campus. Obviously, everyone was asleep at that hour so we simply slept in the vehicles till the sun woke us with a blast of the Arizona heat. We made our way to the Launstein's home where we were welcomed heartily with a great breakfast. The rest of the morning was spent unloading the vehicles and placing our belongings into the apartments assigned to us. We would live in one apartment temporarily and store our extra furnishings in the other. Our worn-out family members, along with some students, helped us with all of this.

That afternoon, Ken and Loma had to leave for Minneapolis and Grandpa Sonmor flew out the next day. The following evening, the college had a banquet with many people attending seeking to publicize the school, the new president and faculty. Steve and I had to sing and had the joy of being accompanied by Rudy Atwood. It was our first time to meet him personally.

The days that followed were mostly spent looking for a home in the area. We also had the joy of being with Dr. Stan Cook and his wife, Ann, for a lovely meal and a great time of reminiscing about our days at Northwestern. Stan

Cook was Vice President in our time at Northwestern and Steve and I had been involved in a radio program he started as well as ministering in music when he went out to speak. Ann also took us to see three prospective homes she knew about.

A few nights later, we had the joy of attending a church in Tempe where, to our surprise, the "Madrigals and Guys" from Faith Academy were singing. These were missionary kids, students at Faith Academy, who had traveled to a few other countries, primarily in Asia but also the U.S. Our kids were so thrilled to see some of their friends again. How good God was to bring friends from the Philippines to this new place. It certainly helped our kids to feel more at home in Arizona. One of Mark's good missionary friends, Lenny Montgomery, was at the concert and now lived in Tempe, so they were excited that they could get together once in a while.

On the way to Arizona, I had been having an intermittent numbness in my left leg, which kept up most of the way. After arriving in Phoenix, it got worse and I also began to feel abdominal pain. The longer we were here, the worse the pain became. I knew something had to be very wrong. Pastor David Hay and his wife, Marita, of Palmcroft Baptist Church, gave us the name of a gynecologist, Dr. Clemenger, with whom I made an appointment. After various tests including an MRI, it was discovered that I had an ovarian cyst about the size of a grapefruit. Of course it had to be surgically removed. It was difficult to enter the hospital so soon after our arrival and especially so near the time we had to begin teaching. Added to that, we still had no real place to call home. Mark, who was still young and always had a tender heart, almost cried when I left for surgery. The girls took it well, all in all. They had weathered many storms before and I knew their faith in God was strong.

The surgery ended up being quite involved. I had to have a total hysterectomy as I not only had the cyst but also had endometriosis, causing me to bleed internally for quite a while. That is probably why I was severely anemic in the Philippines requiring me to have all those iron shots. Hopefully now, some of my physical problems would be over. I was hospitalized for four days when Steve, the kids, and our dog, Sidney, came to take me home. I received a slurpy welcome from Sidney and upon entering the apartment, I noticed on the floor, the "Welcome Home, Mom" written by means of the vacuum cleaner on the carpet. I knew it was my clever son. God's goodness was always there for us in all of the emergencies of life.

During the following days, meals were brought to us from two different churches. Many individuals visited me in the hospital, prayed with me and were such a blessing to our family. Here, in a place where we hardly knew anyone, God provided in unusual ways.

Eventually, I was strong enough to join in the search for a home. We were almost ready to sign papers on a house, when we happened to go by another one that wasn't listed in the realtor's inventory, yet we knew it was for sale. The kids peeked over the wall and noticed a swimming pool and basketball court and immediately thought that would be an ideal place. We were sure it would be out of our reach financially. However, we inquired about it and eventually got to look at it. It had everything we wished for except an office, but we could make it work. It was near the college and close to good schools for the kids. The price was reasonable so we made an offer.

Our offer was accepted and we moved into our home on July 17th with the help of a few students. We were especially grateful for Steve and Tim Okken, missionary kids from Africa, with CBFMS. We had heard of their parents for years and now had the privilege of having them as students. God provided and continually brought familiar people into our lives. Sisters, Charlotte and Phoebe, also flew down from Minneapolis to help us get settled. Tami and Terri were excited when one of their best friends in the Philippines, Susan Romine, came to visit. Susan flew out from Pennsylvania and was with us about a month. I think they spent most of the time swimming. Mark and his friend, Lenny Montgomery, exchanged visits a few times also. The summer might have been quite lonely for our kids if it weren't for these friends from Faith Academy. God met our needs in amazing ways.

Our first Arizona home

Most of the month of August, we had an influx of company. Ken and Loma and their kids came after we got a bit more settled. Our friends, the Siemens, missionaries to Africa came. Many cousins, aunts and uncles came. Grandma Sonmor came along with her sister, Aunt Nora Albrightson. Cousin, Karen Lund, from Seattle, who had gone to college here in Phoenix, got married to Paul Waterford that month and several came for that reason as well.

Toward the end of August, school was starting at the college as well as for the kids. We knew it was going to be a great challenge for all of us. Because Tami and Terri, high school sophomores now, had each other, their adjustment was not too difficult. Mark, however, had a difficult time adjusting for the first couple of weeks. He really missed his friends and his little league teams in Minnesota, but we knew in time, that would change, and soon it did. It wasn't long and many boys his age frequented our home on a regular basis. He became a part of several little league teams and had much excitement winning tournaments, receiving trophies, and finding new friends.

# Chapter 39

## *Life in the Desert*

We began our teaching career at Southwestern Baptist Bible College with excitement, yet fear and trepidation. Though we had both taught before, every situation is different, particularly after serving in another culture. Added to that, we both had to be treated for giardia lamblia, an intestinal parasite. We found the medication very difficult to tolerate, causing jaundice and weakness. I just wasn't able to finish the course of medicine as it was so intolerable. In addition I was still recovering from my hysterectomy, which I discovered was not simply waiting for a wound to heal, it was a matter of hormonal adjustment which for me was the most difficult. I had difficulty sleeping and it also caused anxiety and increased my blood pressure. The estrogen replacement therapy had to be decreased after I ended up in the hospital with very high blood pressure. I'm sure the administration was wondering what they got themselves into for our first weeks of school. Praise the Lord, things eventually evened out for us but there was always pressure, due to preparing for classes we had never taught before.

Along with teaching, a huge responsibility was given to me to train a gospel singing group, which would travel during the summer to represent the college, hoping to recruit new students. This was a particular challenge for me because of being abroad and not really up on the new music available. I spent many days visiting Christian bookstores and exploring music that I thought would be appropriate plus practicing with the interested students every evening. Several faculty members, the president, one board member and I chose the eight singers, and accompanist that we felt would blend and serve well in this capacity. Following that, we had to choose a name for the group so that advertising could be printed and sent out.

I prayed much about a name, went to the Scriptures, and finally came up with the name Chenaniah Singers, based on the man, Chenaniah who was called David's chief musician. "And Chenaniah, leader of the Levites, was instructor in charge of the music, because he was skillful . . ." (I Chronicles 15:22). It took a while before the group decided whether they liked the name but when they understood it, the name stuck for all nineteen years we were at the college. Gradually the group affectionately called it "Chen" and those involved became "the Chen gang."

One of the main challenges for Chenaniah was to prepare for the Conservative Baptist annual meetings. This first year, those meetings were in Estes Park, Colorado. They did amazingly well and we were very proud of them. They traveled throughout the summer in various places in the U.S., particularly in the Southwest. I was not able to travel with them due to family responsibilities but several different faculty men accompanied them. I think Steve had to go a time or two to speak and represent the school.

The first "Chenaniah Singers" of Southwestern College

The second year, Jim Lanning joined our music faculty as the chairman of the department and choral director. He taught various private lessons, basic theory, and art and music appreciation. He then, was able to relieve me of the responsibility of the Chenaniah Singers, as he was free to travel with them. He was an excellent choir director as well as a great trumpeter, which was an added attraction. His wife, Christine, a skilled ventriloquist, was another asset of course. The Lannings did a great deal to build the music program and draw students. Jim also pitched in and got many of the sports programs going at Southwestern.

In the meantime, my responsibilities were increasing as I was asked to serve as Dean of Women and serve on the Dean's Council. I worked with the Women's Auxiliary, which required traveling to churches in the Phoenix area and other cities. Occasionally I was asked to speak to women's groups in various churches and Steve and I together would speak on behalf of missions. As for teaching, I really enjoyed my music theory courses most. It has always been my first love along with singing.

Music is an art, a science, and is mathematical. It is therefore, good for the brain, giving it exercise in many ways. There were four different levels of theory classes, the last two dealt with arranging music for voices and instruments, and dealt with the more advanced nuances involved in composition. It was a thrill to have student James Flamm's composition become one of the songs the choir sang on tour and in their spring concert. There were several exceptionally bright students, which made it very satisfying to teach.

Occasionally, I would have to teach a class that wasn't originally on my teaching schedule as a means of relief for another faculty member. My teaching also included private piano and voice lessons. Consequently recitals were involved as well as final exams or juries as we called them.

A large part of my work at Southwestern had to do with student life. As a dean I was involved in student council, annual awards night, special family dinners, Homecoming festivities, organizing the cheerleaders, and advising the yearbook staff. The latter was a huge job that usually extended into the middle of the summer.

In later years, I taught several courses in women's studies and counseling. By this time I had taken some graduate courses in music at Arizona State University followed by theology classes with emphasis in counseling at Fuller Theological Seminary where I completed a Masters of Arts degree in Theology in 1992. All of this was done without a computer.

Steve's main position was to be Chairman of the Missions Department, but for the first few years, he also took on the job of Dean of Students and Dean of Men, as well as serving on the Dean's Council. He taught several levels of missions courses, anthropology, various Bible classes, Cults and Isms, Evangelism and Baptist History.

Steve also conducted a weeklong missions conference every year with many of our Conservative Baptist missionaries being present throughout the week. This was a very inspirational time for the students as they met with missionaries from various parts of the world. We had one meal during the week with foods from around the world, often in our home, provided by the missionaries. The week usually climaxed with a bonfire where one of the missionaries would share a message or experience, followed by singing and testimonies from the students. Often this week would bring touches of revival with hearts changed, bringing new direction to many.

In the spring of the year, we had an annual missions retreat at Prescott Pines camp in Prescott, Arizona, that was organized by Steve and Rich and Gracie Siemens, our long-time friends from college and seminary days. Rich was the area representative for our mission at this time. Young people from California would join us in this camp. Other missionary guests were a part of this, providing as much exposure to missions as possible. It was a time of learning, fellowship, and a place where lasting decisions were made every year.

Between fall and spring semesters, Steve taught a class in missionary internship where the students would go to an area in Mexico to get some first-hand experience in missionary life with a different language and culture. He also sought to direct students to other mission fields for a summer missionary experience or a short-term mission trip. The Navajo reservation in northern Arizona was also used for this experience at times. These experiences produced many missionaries going out in short-terms as well as becoming career missionaries with CBFMS (now World Venture) or other evangelical missions. At one time

I counted about sixty-four former students who had done either a short or long term of service. It is a thrill for us today to be in touch with many of these through e-mails, Facebook, and some of them personally when they are in our area. Though God chose to bring us home, He also chose to multiply the work in many countries of the world. We can only give Him the glory.

While we were at Southwestern, a new administration/ library building was built, as well as a new gymnasium, chapel, and additional classrooms. Since then new dormitories and a student center have been erected, science building modernized and in general much of the campus has been improved. It has had various administrators and faculty come and go and each one has left his or her mark on the college as well as the lives of the students. Today it is called Arizona Christian University and has its own college level football team which plays other colleges in the Southwest. We pray for the future of this school, that God will continue to use it for His glory.

It's difficult not to mention the trophies of God's grace that emerged from our years at Southwestern. Forty plus students became missionaries and several of my students went on to do graduate work in music and several are worship leaders or are teaching in the field of music.

The following students became full time missionaries during our tenure at Southwestern: Jim and Terri Baugh, Terry and Jeannie Dalrymple, Eric and Sarah Dalrymple, Joanna Beeler, Bill and Nancy McComb, David and Grace Park, Tom and Laura Requadt, Vince and Gail Trujillo, Tim and Jan Okken, Melody Penney, Wayne and Diane Baker, Ben Yazzie, Ray and Theresa Durkin, Eric and Beth Yodis, Rick and Diana Wilson, Joel Madson, Paul Madson, Hugo Venegas, Patrick and Connie Tinkam, Sam and Becky Trommler, Joe and Ramona Steckman,

Ruth Courteol Goodman, Gene Chewning, David Price, Mark Yeager, Paul Sorenson, Gary and Jean Smiddy, Cory and Erica Keith, Tony and Lauren Finch, Tim Fultz, who was killed while serving in Africa, and Christine Ralston. It is impossible to define what these students mean to us.

Several students have excelled in taking leadership in alumnae gatherings such as Mark and Terri Combes, Wayne and Nancy Jones, Allen and Pam Harris, Dave and Debbie Schaeffer, and others. We are so grateful for the labor of love they have put into these endeavors. They have specifically tried to watch when missionaries are home from the field so they can be included along with faculty who are in the area. God has richly blessed Southwestern College and we pray that will continue as it has evolved into Arizona Christian University.

# Chapter 40

## *Family Update*

Basically we spent the last four years of the seventies through 1995 at Southwestern College. Behind the scenes at the college, a great deal of other activity was going on. Our children graduated from high school and all entered college.

Tami and Terri attended Shadow Mountain High School in Phoenix and were very active there particularly in the girls' basketball program. Their basketball team went to state and they were honored with basketball scholarships at Phoenix College in spite of their mere four-feet-eleven height. They graduated from high school in 1979.

Tami and Terri's high school graduation.

Mark was active in football, basketball and band, graduating from junior high the same year Tami and Terri graduated from high school. It was a particularly busy year as it was also Grandma and Grandpa Sonmor's fiftieth wedding anniversary. They and Charlotte and Phoebe were able to be here for the graduations and the anniversary. Other relatives that lived in Phoenix also joined us.

Steve's parent's 50<sup>th</sup> anniversary

The following year, 1980, Steve's sister Phoebe was married on September twentieth, to Mitchell Koentopf of Lakeville, MN. We were disappointed not to be able to attend the wedding as it was just at the beginning of the school year and we couldn't get away. We met Mitch before, but didn't know him well at that time. Sadly, Charlotte, the only attendant for Phoebe had just discovered she had breast cancer. It took away some of the joy that otherwise would have been there. Phoebe and Mitch have never had any children but have always been close to our family. They lived first in the Twin City area of Minnesota, then Pagosa Springs, Colorado; Mesa, Arizona; and presently are in Green Valley, Arizona.

Phoebe and Mitch's wedding

Steve's sister, Charlotte, lived the remainder of her life in the Minneapolis area where she worked for many years at Cargill, Inc. as an office manager. She was a beautiful girl and did some modeling for one of the department stores. She turned down a marriage proposal and passed away in 1987 from the cancer that she so bravely fought for seven years.

Uncle Walter Olson, who married Aunt Hazel, also died that year on March eighth, just about a month prior to Charlotte's death. Steve and I were able to be in Minnesota during that time, never expecting the sudden heart attack of Walter. We had the joy of having Aunt Hazel and Walter spend vacations with us in Phoenix several times. After Walter's death, we had Aunt Hazel spend every winter with us in Phoenix.

In 1980, Tami and Terri were ready to begin college and wanted to continue to play basketball. They started their college careers at Phoenix Community College where they had basketball scholarships. They also enrolled in some of the basic college courses at Southwestern College. Eventuallly they were full-time students at Southwestern majoring in Elementary Education. At first, there was no sports program for girls at Southwestern, therefore, they chose to become cheerleaders for the guys' team and participated in intramural sports, the foreign missions fellowship, yearbook staff, and other activities. They were privileged to go on a sports mission to South America where they played basketball in Argentina, Brazil, and Chile. This provided them with many unique experiences. Both graduated with honors in 1984. Steve was privileged to speak at their Baccalaureate.

The twins enjoyed cheerleading

The twins' college graduation

The girls had various jobs during college and purchased their own cars. The job that stands out most was working in a Deli area of the Alpha Beta Grocery store. Each was at a different location. They had many interesting stories of the deliverymen wondering how they could be two places at once. It was common for them to be mistaken for each other. This has continued to happen all through their lives. When their own children were very young they were often confused as to who was their mommie.

Mark graduated from Shadow Mountain High School in 1983 where he was involved in track and basketball. His interest in art was discovered at a very young age and it has continued throughout the years. He won the award for being the outstanding art student of the year in high school and we were invited to a special dinner, in downtown Phoenix, where he received this award in the presence of school officials and TV newscasters. He was given an art scholarship to Northern Arizona University; however, he decided to come to Southwestern as he had already started taking private trumpet lessons there with Jim Lanning.

Mark was president of his class for several years, and student body president at Southwestern. With his art ability, he designed several of the yearbook covers as well as other projects. He played on the basketball team, sang bass in the choir and Chenaniah Singers. He took two mission trips to the Orient with groups from the college involved in music and drama called "Tradewinds" and "Masterpeace." He particularly enjoyed taking Bibles into China and climbing Mt. Fuji in Japan. Another high point was going back to the Philippines where he grew up. This was an added blessing in that his future bride was with him on this trip and though they had no definite plans at that time, it gave her some insight into his background. Mark graduated in 1989 as a missions major and took an additional year to take some music theory and travel again with Chenaniah. He was awarded outstanding male student of the year in his senior year.

Mark's High School Graduation

One of the Chenaniah groups Mark participated in

Basketball buddies relax at our house after practice

Mark's College graduation

Following Southwestern, Mark took some art courses at Scottsdale Community College. During high school and college, Mark worked as a technical illustrator for Integrated Circuit Engineering in Scottsdale. He was so fortunate to have a job of this caliber at that young age.

Terri became engaged during college and was married a week after graduation. On May 4, 1984, at Palmcroft Baptist Church, she married Ed Godoy, a fellow graduate of Southwestern. He was a former football player, singer, class president and student body president as well as one of the photographers for the yearbook. Both Steve and I had the privilege of having him in our classes. They had a lovely wedding with many family members involved. Ed's family and friends came from Yakima, Washington, and our relatives came from Minnesota and Wisconsin.

Terri and Ed began their married life in Ed's hometown of Yakima, Washington where he worked in a family business called Yakima Electronics. Eventually, he was called back to Phoenix to work for a building contractor in Mesa where they lived. On August 15, 1985, their first daughter, Jamie Susan was born. What an adorable child with her dark brown hair and brown eyes. The following year, they moved to Washington again and back to the Phoenix area in 1988 when Ed was called to be the youth pastor at Palmcroft Baptist Church. On January 5, 1988, blond and blue-eyed Janae Elizabeth was born. We enjoyed these little sisters so much.

During this time, Tami had begun teaching and coaching Basketball in several schools. Eventually, she began teaching sixth grade in a Paradise Valley school while coaching girls' basketball at Paradise Valley High School. She had dated many different Christian guys but never seemed to find the one that was just right for her. She was very successful in coaching, however, and had a team that went to state twice.

Terri and Ed were having a good time ministering at Palmcroft with the youth and during this time the pastor resigned and Palmcroft had to search for a new pastor. My husband, Steve was on the pulpit committee and was very interested in securing Pastor Don Engram from Elyria, Ohio, who was hesitant to leave his large church there. However, he eventually accepted the call to come and we were very pleased to have Don and Sharon when they arrived in 1988.

After hearing Pastor Engram preach, I remember Tami saying, "I wish he had a son." Soon we heard tragic news. The Engrams did have a son named Steve whose wife had given birth to a baby boy and was not responding after having a stroke caused by toxemia. We all joined in prayer for the situation and soon we heard that Steve Engram's wife, Pam, had passed away, leaving Steve to raise his infant son. I recall praying, *Lord, I don't know what this young man is like but I know he eventually will need someone to raise this baby and I don't even know if he would be a good match for our Tami and I also know this would be a difficult situation, but I pray that if this man would be good for Tami, you can work out what is best.* In the meantime Sharon Engram knew Terri and knew Tami was her twin and eventually told Steve about Tami. Of course Steve wasn't ready to think about anyone else for a while.

Eventually Palmcroft called Steve to come to work as pastor to the college-career group as well as leading evangelism. Eventually, months and months later, God miraculously led them together. I remember Tami was concerned about whether Steve would like sports, especially basketball. She only thought of him as a preacher and he is a great preacher. She found out later he was just as interested in basketball as she was. I cannot go into all of the interesting details of this love affair but God led them together in a marvelous way. Tami had to wait until she was twenty-eight, five years after her twin sister's marriage, but God knew who was best for her. Tami started caring for little Jamie Boy, as we called him, since we also had a Jamie Girl! He started calling her "mommie" before Tami and Steve were married which took place, December 1, 1989, and the wedding of course was also held at Palmcroft. Both fathers officiated and we had the reception in the new gymnasium at Southwestern.

By the time they were married, Jamie was a toddler and was able to dress in a little tuxedo and march out with the bride and groom as they were pronounced husband and wife. For several months both Tami and Terri's husbands were on staff at the same church. It wasn't long, however, when Ed was called back to Yakima where he worked in Yakima Electronics again and later in construction of new homes in Mesa, Arizona.

December 28, 1990, we had another Christmas

wedding as Mark married Carolyn Fadely, a lovely girl from Page, Arizona. She came to Southwestern on a music scholarship. Carolyn has a lovely voice and was an Elementary Education major, involved in choir, and also a cheerleader. She worked as a student secretary for the academic dean. Carolyn had also been a part of one of the trips to the Orient with Mark and they got acquainted during Mark's senior year at Southwestern. She had one stipulation for a husband—that he would get along with her dad and that he would like fishing. Well, that one wasn't difficult for Mark as he has always loved to fish and her dad, Gary, was the most likeable fun guy you could ever meet and was a fine Christian teacher and leader. They were also married at Palmcroft. Special features in the ceremony included Carolyn's dad, Gary Fadely, singing *The Lord's Prayer*, Mark and Carolyn singing to each other, and having Grandpa Sonmor as the best man though he was in his eighties at the time. Grandpa always meant so much to Mark. Steve of course officiated as usual.

Grandma Sonmor, by this time was in a rest home due to her failing heart and was unable to be at the wedding. She was thrilled, however, that her husband could go and be a vital part of it. She passed away the following year at age eighty-three on November 21, 1991 with Aunt Hazel following her in death one month later on December 13th at age eighty-four. Life was changing for all of us as we saw loved ones pass away and we became empty nesters.

Tami and Steve had their first child together on September 30, 1991; Jeremy Joseph was born after Tami was put on several months of bed rest. JJ, as we've called him, was pretty small but healthy. He had blond hair and big brown eyes, a very special little guy with a big heart. He was born C-section and Jamie Boy was so thrilled that he had a brother. Each of these grandchildren is special in their own way and mean so much to us.

On April 12, 1994, Mark and Carolyn had their first child, Taylor Kent, a little blond curly head with big brown eyes. His hair turned darker as he got older. They were now living in Salt Lake City, Utah, where Mark took a youth pastorate and later an artist job for San Segal, doing art for nature type T-shirts, while also getting a degree in art at the University of Utah.

On August 13, 1995, Mom's youngest brother, Joseph Feldhahn, passed away at ninety-three years of age. He was a dear man who was especially good to us as children as well as remembering us with gifts at Christmas and at our weddings. He never married but worked hard at manual labor all of his life. He was especially good to Mom and Aunt Louise.

One Sunday noon, in 1995, we got the surprise of our lives when Tami and Terri told us they were both pregnant and due about two weeks apart. Then we found out Carolyn was also pregnant a few weeks later. It was quite the year! Terri had her first boy, Edward Jordan (who goes by Jordan) on August 9th. He has dark hair with brown eyes very similar to his sister, Jamie. Tami had Kylee Rae, blond and blue eyed, her first girl on August 30th, and Carolyn had Cady (pronounced Kaydee) also blond and beautiful green eyes on September 23rd. Mark loves the place called Cady in Wisconsin where Steve and I were born and they decided to name this baby girl after that place. All went quite well, except Tami had a rough time with Kylee, having to have another C-section at the last minute as her former scar ruptured and caused the bladder to start to rupture also. Praise the Lord things worked out and it has been fun having three cousins the same age. It was a scary time for son-in-law Steve having gone through what he did with his first wife, Pam.

God blessed our children, and us and continues to lead as these children have grown up. We experienced the normal ups and downs during their teenage years, they certainly were not perfect and there were days when we as parents had to learn important lessons along with them. However, I thank God for His guidance as we met each night in family devotions unless they weren't home for some reason. Several of their friends joined with us at times and some of them came to know Christ during those years, not because of us, but because of the witness of the kids. We can only give God the glory. I attribute it to God's mercy and grace in answering our prayers. There is no greater joy than to have your children walk with God. Neither is there any greater pain than losing a child to the wicked ways of the evil one.

Steve and Tami Engram's family
Steve, JJ, Jamie in rear, Tami with Peter,
Lydia with Leanor and Kylee

Ed and Terri Godoy family
Alex and Janae Klein, Jordan, Jamie, Terri and Ed Godoy

Mark and Carolyn Sonmor family
Left to right – Abigail, Taylor, Cady, Mark,
Carolyn, Chandler, and Maggie

The newest family member born to Taylor and Abigail
Olivia Taylor Sonmor

# Chapter 41

*Testing the Waters*

During the summer of 1979, Steve was invited to fill in for missionary, David Swinehart who pastored Bayview Baptist Church in Guam. He was gone from June 20, through August 5. He never expected to minister to the people with Transworld Radio who broadcast the Gospel into China from Guam but he was able to minister directly to the staff on one occasion and found typical missionary problems among them. They were a very talented group and a real blessing to be with. The director of the Guam group at that time, went on to become the overall director of Transworld Radio. The Conservative Baptist Church on Guam was established originally for ministry to the G.I.'s at the church and the servicemen's center.

Guam continues to be a conglomeration of people from several islands in the Micronesia area with various religious backgrounds as well as a large group of Filipinos who are living and working on the island. One of the purposes for Steve going there that summer was to test it out to see if he could stand the climate of Guam better than the Philippines. He was okay until the last week when he began to get sick.

When he got on the plane to head back to the mainland, he was so thankful for space enough to stretch out and sleep. It helped him to restore his equilibrium but he also began to realize that ministry on Guam was not going to be possible either.

Steve knew the ministry at the college was great but it was difficult to accept the fact that our missionary service in the Philippines was over. In the summer of 1981, he raised enough support financially to make a trip back to the Philippines for a little over two months to see if he could take the tropics once again.

He was met at the airport by Filipinos that were like family and it was a joy to see them but within three days he got sick again and if his ticket had allowed, he probably would have come home as quickly as possible but he was stuck for two months. God, however, had a plan and purpose in that time even though he was sick off and on the entire time.

He went to Iloilo on the island of Panay to stay with some relatives of members in the Makati church. Before we left the Philippines it was our desire to see a Conservative Baptist church started in Iloilo but going back gave him a better perspective regarding the possibility. Their main contact there was related to a member of our church in Makati. She and her husband had a friend whom they really felt would be open to receiving Christ and was in a desperate spiritual condition. Years before, this woman was known in the area as a beauty queen. A very wealthy Chinese businessman wanted her to become his business partner in marriage, so she left her husband and married the businessman. Things went along fine for many years until the ravages of time began to gnaw away at her appearance and her husband decided he didn't want her anymore.

She still had a house and income but she also had a very lonely heart and a desperate soul. Steve and his friends went there one morning and she invited Steve to see her prayer room. He related to her that she needed to know Christ as her personal Savior and explained to her that God doesn't hear our prayers if we harbor sin in our hearts. This was very unsettling to her. Soon she prayed with Steve and asked Jesus into her heart and life.

One evening as Steve was in the home of the people he was staying with, they served a delicious meal with shellfish after which they had a Bible study together. In the midst of it Steve was struck with diarrhea and vomiting requiring him to rush to the bathroom and retire early to bed. Jake Toews, the missionary who was with him, finished the Bible study for him. It was very frustrating for Steve to have to leave there, as there were so many great contacts. He would have liked to stay and start a church. After being so sick, however, he knew he wasn't going to be able to go back to the Philippines to stay.

Tony Pezzota, a former priest who had been sent from Rome to the Philippines in years past, was also in the area. He and Steve were able to minister together. Tony authored the book, *Truth Encounter*, that deals with Catholicism and the Holy Scriptures. He was now married and he and his wife came to Bacolod City on the island of Negros. There was a group of young Catholic seminarians that joined them for breakfast to see why Tony had left the priesthood. Tony was not antagonistic and he was very gracious in how he dealt with these men.

Steve was able to travel north with Tony and his wife to see some of the places where Tony ministered when he was a priest there. They also visited a group of Christians who were having a baptismal service in a river that day.

The people Steve stayed with went out of their way for him and took him to see a Bible school some distance away. They had to take an old jeep, as it was many miles out of Bacolod. There were students and some faculty but no library. They had a child's set of encyclopedias, the director actually had an old typewriter, and they received gifts from various people to supply rice and vegetables but they didn't have a consistent, balanced diet. The students were so hard up they had to plant rice themselves on the land that was allotted at the school and take air rifles to shoot birds in order to get a little bit of protein. Steve said they were an amazing bunch of people. He spent a whole afternoon ministering to them and he will never forget that Bible school. It was truly being run on a shoestring but the dedication of the students was phenomenal.

Steve also visited with our good friends, Bob and Marge Skivington, formerly in Laguna Province on Luzon, who had relocated in Davao. Steve was able to minister to a bunch of nurses there. Bob had purchased a plot of land on the edge of Davao that he hoped would be a good place for a Bible College. While they were together, a young man came from the mountains where fighting was going on between the guerillas and the government forces. The man's wife had just been killed by the guerillas. There were many difficult situations like this going on in that area.

When leaving the Philippines, Steve also stopped in Hawaii and visited with students at International Bible College. One of the young men took him to the Bible camp for the church, where he got to minister to the students at the camp.

It was a difficult trip, yet profitable while he was there. Having diarrhea for a month after his return, however, showed him he could never return. As he arrived at Sky Harbor Airport, he looked like "warmed over death," as we say, and I could see that he had lost a lot of weight. I was very concerned about him.

While Steve was gone, the kids and I attacked our house, which we had never really been able to settle completely due to the rigid schedule at the college. We cleaned every room and closet, painted walls, refinished furniture and the home had a complete makeover (as much as we could afford). It was mostly done with hard physical work and it was a thrill to have it looking good to welcome Steve back home. I was so grateful to my kids for their hard work and they were excited to see the results of their labors.

We had several difficulties while Steve was gone such as car troubles and various decisions related to our home, and the kids' jobs. However, the incident that was most difficult was discovering that someone had shot a bullet through our large living room window. The bullet went right through the living and dining room and lodged in the doorway between the dining room and kitchen. It was a bit frightening to be there without my man. We never heard the shot and didn't discover it till the next morning. I had missionaries from Brazil, parents of two students at the college, in for fellowship the night before. Fortunately it happened after they left or they would have been sitting right in the line of fire. We of course had to call the police, get insurance estimates and get the window and doorway repaired and new draperies as it had ripped right through. God was good though and gave us peace even in that dire situation. I thank the Lord we never had anything like that occur again. For fear of worrying Steve, I didn't tell him about this until he came home.

In 1995, God seemed to show us that our time at the college was over. We had thoroughly enjoyed our years there but we were nearing retirement and Steve felt like he would like to try pastoring again prior to total retirement. Therefore, when approached about pastoring at the First Baptist Church in Page, Arizona, he was willing to consider it.

Page is located in Northern Arizona on Lake Powell and is surrounded by various Navajo villages. Page was an interesting place, being over one hundred miles from any city of size. There was a small airport but very little shopping other than Wal-Mart and a few Western type stores, two grocery stores, sporting goods stores and several restaurants. It was a place that attracted many tourists due to Lake Powell and its close proximity to the Grand Canyon.

The Page Church Campus

Carolyn's parents, Gary and Nancy Fadely lived in Page where they were both schoolteachers. Gary was also our choir director at the church. It was great to get to know them better while we were there. I was primarily involved with the women's ministry and choir.

While there in Page I discovered a lump in my breast, which required that I have a biopsy. I was of course frightened and prayed much about it asking for God's peace and relief from anxiety. One night, particularly, I felt troubled and prayed for peace. Suddenly I remembered I had been hit there when a metal file cabinet drawer slid open and hit me in that very spot where the lump was located. It was God's way of assuring me. I had totally forgotten the incident even though I remember at the time thinking, *Wow that was not a good place to get hit!*

Praise the Lord; I went into the surgery knowing in my heart that it would be benign, which it was. God is so good in all things if we will just ask.

Mark and Carolyn were still living in Salt Lake City, so the drive to see them wasn't real far and they of course could see both sets of parents when they came to Page. Grandpa Sonmor also spent months at a time with us there. He enjoyed the scenery and getting to see family whenever possible. We were privileged to have our whole family there one Christmas where some participated musically in our Christmas program where we again used the drama I had written so many years ago while teaching in Dallas.

We learned a lot during our time at Page and God gave souls and many were baptized but God didn't have us there for a long time. It soon became clear that God was leading us back to the Phoenix area where we got involved in a group called Life Partners and Christ Quest Institute begun by Ken and Nancy Nair. I learned of this program while working on my Master's Degree. I used one of Ken's books as a reference for one of my assignments. I felt we needed to get into this ministry, as we desperately needed refreshment from burnout, where we could take in the teaching rather than continually giving out to others. It is basically a marriage enrichment study where participants, particularly men, are taught how to brcome Christ-like. We studied for three years and then helped to facilitate discussion groups. We appreciated so much what God did in our lives through Christ Quest Institute.

Toward the end of our time at Southwestern College, I was beginning to have digestive issues, which continually got worse while in Page. I had gall bladder surgery while at Southwestern but it didn't take care of the entire problem. It is something I may fight the rest of my life. I am not sure if it has resulted from all the dysentery I had in the Philippines but it seems to have been my "thorn in the flesh" for at least twenty-four years.

Gary and Nancy Fadely left Page to accept teaching jobs in the West Phoenix area and settled in the Rancho Santa Fe Subdivision of Avondale. That was now where Tami and Steve were living. We hadn't planned it this way, but God also led us to that same subdivision where we are still located. We are just a short distance from Fadely's and are serving together in Desert Springs Community Church that has grown from fifty people to about 1300. Steve and Tami have served as pastor and wife in that church for almost twenty-three years at this time. It has moved to larger locations twice and is a story of God's amazing grace. Desert Springs has also started a daughter church in a growing area. Son-in-law, Steve, is also the Southwest Church Connection Regional Executive for our fellowship of churches.

Mark and Carolyn have had two more children, Maggie Rebecca, born January 13, 1998, an adorable, brown-eyed brunette and Chandler Stephen, blond and blue-eyed, born August 5, 2002. Mark and family now live in Grand Junction, Colorado, where he has his own graphics art business but continues to work for Alpha Omega Institute, a creation research institute, which was the reason he first went to Grand Junction. He also taught art and graphics to the business students at the University there and has several clients with interesting projects of various types to keep him from getting bored in life and expand his knowledge in art. Carolyn has homeschooled all the kids.

Terri and Ed are back in Yakima, Washington, where they've built a new home near the schools for the children. Ed's office for Greenway Transportation is in their home and Terri has ministered for many years as Director of Children's Ministry at their church. Ed has been very involved in teaching adults, singing solos and in various music groups. He has often designed and built props for Terri's children's musicals. We never realized all of the artistic talent he has until recent years.

New developments continue within our family and ministry, which you will see as our story continues. Hopefully seeing God's hand in the movement of our lives, you will also see His hand in your own lives. That is His desire for all of His children.

# Chapter 42

*Retirement Years*

We moved from Page to Avondale, a suburb of Phoenix, in August 1997. Since we didn't know for sure what we would be doing, Tami and Steve offered to have us stay with them for a while. We arrived just in time to celebrate our fortieth wedding anniversary. The kids had planned a lovely celebration with family flying in from Minnesota and other areas. How grateful we were for that time together as it was the last time we would see my sister-in-law, Loma, who passed away from cancer on November fifth of that year. I was able to spend about two weeks with brother Ken after her funeral and since then he often spends time with us in Arizona during the winter months. God has gifted him in art and he has done charcoal drawings of many of our kids and grandkids. He has never remarried but has had many lovely Christian lady friends.

Never would we have imagined that we would be staying with Tami and Steve for almost five months. Jamie gave up his room for us and joined JJ in his room. We found it difficult to settle in anywhere until we knew for sure what we were going to do. We thought perhaps a pastorate would open up for us but we found it was a bit more difficult now that we were older. We were involved as an interim pastor at Palo Verde Baptist Church, west of Avondale, for a short time but they did have a new pastor coming. Steve eventually took a secular job for an air conditioning firm starting out in the office and eventually driving a truck to deliver construction materials for the installation of air conditioning units.

Eventually, we decided to purchase our first new home, that is, one where we could choose the carpets, countertops etc. This was in the same subdivision as Tami and Steve and the Fadelys. The housing market was good at this time and after much prayer, we felt God was leading us in this. It was a home adequate for us, not large or pretentious but everything we needed. It has proven to be a step in the right direction.

Our home in Avondale

For seven years, our Monday evenings were involved in Life Partners which I mentioned in the last chapter. We were also involved in Desert Springs Community Church, located at that time in Glendale. Tami and Steve left their ministry at Palmcroft Baptist Church to come to the aid of Desert Springs, which at that time was struggling to stay alive.

Along with our various duties at the church, we soon got involved in a Philippine Bible study in East Phoenix. Tony Pezzota, the former priest, had befriended some folk there who wanted to have a Bible study. Tony had heard we were in the area and recommended they contact us to see if we were interested. We carried on this study every Saturday evening for about sixteen years. It was a thrill to be able to continue to see Filipinos come to Christ here in our homeland. We were able to use our Tagalog some, however, these people came from various islands in the Philippines and were not all Tagalog speakers. We even had weddings, baptisms, and funerals among these dear people. We met in various homes in Mesa, Gilbert, Chandler, and Apache Junction. It was a long drive for us especially on Saturday nights but it seemed to work best for them. The problem was waking up early Sunday morning for Steve to teach his adult Sunday school class which he has also done consistently for close to twenty years. After all these years of ministry, he has really found that teaching is the special gift God has given him. He enjoys the study and preparation as well as the class interaction. As a result his Sunday school class has been very special to us—somewhat of a support group, you might say. Steve has always been active in witnessing and is one of the best soul winners I've ever known. I thank God for a man of integrity and a concerned heart for others over the years.

One of many Philippine Bible studies in East Phoenix

As for me, for several years I edited the Women's Inspirational Network, a paper for the Conservative Baptists in the Southwest. I was just beginning to learn the basics of computers so it was quite a challenge. Now, however, information is no longer sent by mail, therefore, newsletters have pretty much been discontinued. The church prayer chain, women's Bible study, and choir occupied my time in the past and presently I continue to head up the church prayer chain, have a prayer group in our home related to our women's ministry and other needs of the church. I am involved in Bible studies as I am able.

Steve eventually left the air-conditioning company planning on full retirement, but soon was asked to do maintenance work at the church, which was then located in Litchfield Park where we took over a former Catholic church. He took real pride in keeping up the church grounds and found it to be good bodily exercise. The only difficulty was the excessive heat in the summer time. I was worried about him working so hard in the heat. Eventually when the church moved to the present location, a few blocks further west on the same street, it was necessary to hire a company to take care of the maintenance since the greater acreage and larger building required more work.

As the church grew, Pastor Steve, our son-in-law, found it very difficult to keep up with all of the necessary visitation, so the church board hired my husband, Steve, to come on the church staff as pastor of visitation. He dearly loves it and God has really used him in that position. It is a thrill to see how God uses all of our former experiences to prepare us for things we never dreamed we would do and we have realized that God saves some of those things for our "golden" years to give us a bit of significance and joy rather than drying up on the vine, so to speak. Our church has what we call "Connect Groups" which gather weekly in homes where we are able to get to know each other better, pray, and fellowship together. We have been leading one of those groups for about twelve years and just recently turned it over to a younger couple that is doing a great job.

Grandpa Sonmor spent several winters with us ever since we lived near the college. He stayed with us also while we lived in Avondale as well. He divided his time between Phoebe and Mitch and us. He had such a wonderful disposition and tried very hard not to be a burden. However, it was very difficult at the end when he needed care in the middle of the night and Steve had to be at work very early. Phoebe had to eventually take time off from her job and he passed away at their home in Pagosa Springs, CO on December 3, 1999. He was ninety-six.

My sister, Hildi, had open-heart surgery in the year 2000. We were so grateful after all her years of weakness that Mayo Clinic said they could do the surgery and she would be healed. We were so thankful and hopeful. She came through the surgery well but from then on she had dementia due to having insufficient oxygen going to her brain. She lived until 2009 but never had the kind of life she desired and her last years were difficult for her husband Bill and daughter Darla. She did, however, get to enjoy Darla's marriage to Mark Hetchler and subsequently their six children whom she loved dearly.

In 2002, we received word that Northwestern College was going to have a great celebration for it's one-hundredth anniversary. Several friends contacted us about going, which we wanted to do but Steve had not been feeling well. He contacted his doctor who sent him to a gastroenterologist. The doctor was very concerned and requested him to have an endoscopy since they had found a mass on his liver. The doctor felt sure it was liver cancer. We of course were very concerned and knew we couldn't make a trip to Minnesota if this was the case. While Steve was having the endoscopy, I sat in the waiting room, praying and reading the book, *Prisoners of Hope*, written by the girls who were imprisoned by the Taliban in Afghanistan. As I read, I came upon these words: "For we would not want you to be unaware, Brethren, of the affliction we experienced in Asia. For we were so utterly burdened beyond our strength that we despaired of life itself" (2 Corinthians 1:8 ESV). It was like I was pricked in my spirit and I couldn't help but wonder if God was telling me to remember the afflictions we had in Asia (the Philippines), and for Steve, it involved the liver. Yet, I knew he had that all checked out at Mayo Clinic. Could it have gotten worse? I remember coming home and praying through my tears to spare Steve from this awful disease but if He didn't, to please help me learn to love God more and know of His love for me. I knew I couldn't go through this without a very personal sense of God's presence.

The following day we went to the pulmonologist as the doctor felt if Steve had liver cancer, he could very likely have it in his lungs. On the way to the doctor I felt so desperate and I remember praying, *"Lord, please help this lung doctor to give us some hope about the liver."* I know now, that was sort of a silly prayer but somehow I wasn't worried about the lungs, I *was* concerned about the liver. What would the lung doctor know about the liver? However, when Steve finished his exam and we were walking to the car, he said, "You know, that doctor told me not to worry that much about the liver. He said, "That's probably related to that amoebic dysentery and hepatitis you had in the Philippines." Wow! I almost shouted for joy. We didn't know anything for certain but I believe God was giving me hope. I felt certain that he didn't have liver cancer. I couldn't sleep that night, this time, not because of fear, but because of joy. I had to stay up and just praise the Lord for his kindness in answering my prayer. *I had simply prayed for this lung doctor to give us hope regarding the liver and he did.* What a great and personal God we have, and it doesn't matter how foolish or small our prayer might be. We still had to wait for several days for the final word, but I knew what the answer would be. The answer did come and he was free of any cancer. Out of curiosity I called Mayo Clinic in Minnesota to get Steve's records on his former liver biopsy. It was the same then as it was now. Nothing had changed. It was still from "the affliction he had in Asia." I think they called it an "angio hematoma."

We decided to make the trip to Minnesota via Colorado where we visited Mark and Carolyn and a naturopathic doctor. The doctor gave Steve something that made him feel better within a few days and we were able to enjoy the one-hundredth anniversary of Northwestern College and renew fellowship with many of our friends. Several of the couples were able to get together at our home a year or so later. Dick and Patti Wiens and Dick and Zoma Edstrom wintered in the Phoenix area so we were able to have great fellowship. If we had not gone to this reunion, we wouldn't have known they were here. How marvelous and good are the blessings from His hand.

All of my siblings have seen blessings in their families as well. Here is a peek at the growth of their families:

Bill, Hildi, and Darla Mann

Darla and Mark Hetchler family
Ryan, Emily, Allison, Mark, Darla with Jacob, Caleb and
Anna in front with Bill Mann (Grandpa) in the back

Ken and Loma Haglund family
Lynette, Ken, Loma, Lori, and Kevin, Brian Nibbe in back

Brian and Lynette Nibbe's family
Arezoo, Brian Jr., Lynette, Brent, Dory, Brian,
Sr., Bradley. Brandon, and Delia

David and Lori Drury family
David, Hunter, Colton in rear, Lori, Lauren &
Trevor Koch with Jude Koch and Alyssa Drury

Kevin and Suzanne Haglund family
Ellie, Suzanne, Kevin, Ethan, and Sarah

# Chapter 43

## *More Trauma*

As we've aged, I guess it's normal to experience some additional problems and gradually, we lost more of our loved ones. My mother's sister, our dear Aunt Louise, who had had been such a vital part of our lives, passed away at ninety-three years of age on June 20, 2003. She was very special in my life. I'm thankful I took her advice in writing.

Aunt Louise and Marilyn at her 90th birthday

In 2007, we celebrated our Fiftieth wedding anniversary with a cruise with friends, a large celebration at our church and a weekend with all the immediate family at a lovely lodge in Greer, Arizona. The kids presented us with a lovely, enlarged family picture which now hangs in our family room. It's amazing how fast all the grandkids have grown up so that we now need another which is more up-to-date.

Front Row: Cady Sonmor, Jeremy Engram, Marilyn holding Chandler Sonmor, Janae Godoy, Taylor Sonmor Second Row: Maggie Sonmor, Kylee Engram, Steve Sonmor, Third Row: Carolyn Sonmor, Tami Engram, Terri Godoy, Jordan Godoy, Jamie Godoy, Back Row: Mark Sonmor, James Engram, Steve Engram, Ed Godoy.

A few years ago both Steve and I got pneumonia at the same time. We were thankful again for Tami and Steve and our Sunday school class who came with meals and did errands for us. It took us a long time to get our strength back, but praise God, we did recover.

The year 2014 was perhaps the most difficult year we

have had. My heart would occasionally beat very fast but upon examination by the doctor, it would appear to be normal. Anxiousness would cause my blood pressure to rise, and I would go through times of terrible weakness. With each visit to the E.R., I would find either a lack of potassium or sodium, which at times would require a night in the hospital for IV treatments in whatever I was lacking. This kept happening over and over again. Each time I thought I wouldn't even make it to the hospital. I was afraid I wouldn't be able to finish this book that I believe God wanted me to write. I said, *God, I thought you wanted me to write this book for you, but it's up to you. I know unless you give me strength and renewal, I can't do it. I just pray for your will to be done.* Each time He raised me up. God had previously given me these words: "Do not cast me away when I am old; do not forsake me when my strength is gone . . . Even when I am old and gray, do not forsake me, O God, until I declare your power to the next generation, your might to all who are to come. . . .Though you have made me see troubles, many and bitter, you will restore my life again (Psalm 71:9,18,20 NIV).

I clung to those verses as I have written these words, but one day I felt I just couldn't go on. I prayed, *Lord, I just don't think I can do this. Please help me, I need encouragement and hope."* I sat on my bed and wept, crying out to God. He seemed to tell me to Read Psalm 119. I determined to read every word of that longest chapter in the Bible. There were many verses that encouraged me. Then I came to a portion where I lacked concentration. I paused, reading it over and over seeking to get the meaning. God knew I needed these words: "Remember your word to your servant, for you have given me hope. My comfort in my suffering is this: Your promise preserves my life" (Psalm 119:49 NIV). Then I realized God gave me a promise in Psalm 71 not to forsake me when I was old and gray and that I would be able to declare His power to the next generation. This was to be my promise of hope. I found that being obedient with writing gave me joy and hope for each day.

I began to realize that with my digestive issues, I often lost my necessary electrolytes. I am gradually learning how to keep in better balance with an electrolyte supplement. Praise God, He knows what we need. I still depend on Him, for He is the Great Physician.

I was doing quite well when we found Steve had to have part of his enlarged prostate removed. He was scheduled for surgery and the night before, we had gone for a long walk, after which I decided to take a birthday card over to my next-door neighbor, Terri Wright. We had a short visit and as I was ready to leave her home, I got a terrible pain in my chest and everything went black. I felt like I was swirling into a dark hole and my heart was racing. Terri's husband walked me home and Steve rushed me to the E.R. where a crew descended on me, stopped my heart and started it again. They gave me a beta-blocker blood pressure pill to keep my heart in a steady rhythm. They called it Supraventricular Tachycardia. I was put in the hospital for two days and found that I had to have an ablation with a specialist who dealt with the electrical system of the heart. I was blessed to have one of the best doctors available for that procedure.

Steve, however, had to have his scheduled surgery. We were both in the hospital at the same time but in different wings of the hospital. I got home one day before Steve and had the ablation done about a week later as an outpatient without a single pain or fear. Tami and Steve took care of all of the logistics and she was the one who had to be with me for the procedure. God provided two Christian Filipino nurses to care for me and provide great conversation for me while I waited to be released.

Again, God showed His love and care. Since then I have had what they call Premature Ventricular Contractions (PVC's) where one beat may come early and one is delayed. It is rather annoying but they tell me not to be concerned with it. I rarely notice it anymore.

Steve had a long recovery that included getting rid of an infection. Yet even that, God very uniquely took care of. He very recently had to have this same prostate surgery over again as the first one grew back. This one, so far has gone much better and we are trusting the Lord for a complete recovery. Doctors recently checked out some nodules in his lungs but two biopsies proved no cancer. He is also facing another hernia surgery so we are again looking to God for His healing hand that we may continue to serve Him in our sunset years.

During these last years, many changes have come about in our family. Mark and Carolyn's oldest son, Taylor, was married in August, 2014, to Abigail Cook. They have made their home in Grand Junction, Colorado and are the proud parents of a beautiful baby girl, Olivia Taylor.

We also saw our first grandson Jamie Engram get married to Lydia Ley with little Peter Ray joining their family two years later. On March 1, 2016 they had a precious baby girl, Leanor Lynne.

In October, 2015, we flew to Yakima, Washington, to attend Terri and Ed's daughter Janae's marriage to Alex Klein, a fine young man. They both played soccer at different universities and met on a mission together in Jamaica. Both have jobs in Seattle.

Terri and Ed's oldest, Jamie Godoy, is involved in music and working in Nashville, Tennessee, while their youngest, Jordan, is an electrical engineering student at George Fox University in Newberg, Oregon.

Jamie and Lydia Engram are on staff at our church

where Jamie is the worship leader and they work with the college-age youth. JJ (Jeremy) Engram has graduated from Moody Bible Institute in Spokane, Washington and working at Dutch Bros. Coffee, has taken two mission trips to Japan and one to the Philippines. He also worked with the Jr. High Youth in our church. He spent about a month in the Philippines recently as he took a trip with his parents and Terri and Ed. He is seriously considering missionary service. Kylee Engram is a senior at Grand Canyon University studying Elementary Education. She has earned a scholarship through cheerleading.

Mark's daughters, Cady and Maggie both attended Colorado Mesa University. Cady recently married Christian Bell, a fine Christian young man. Maggie is taking her basic classes at the local university and would really like to go to Bible College. She is interested in missions. Chandler, their youngest, fifteen is still in home school with his mom and involved in the home school co-op. That pretty much brings the grandchildren up-to-date.

Steve and I are thankful we still have each other and one sibling—my brother Ken and his sister Phoebe. Ken and I have always been close. He lives in Apple Valley, Minnesota, and tries to visit as often as possible during the winter months. Phoebe and Mitch are still in Arizona but recently moved to Green Valley, near Tucson so they are a bit further away than they were in Mesa.

We have been privileged to live during some of the greatest times in America and presently, we are presented with some of the most challenging times. We are excited to see what God is going to do and we of course are looking forward to that greatest day of all—when we will hear that trumpet call and hear Jesus' words, "Come up here." It could be very soon. I hope each one of you is ready. It doesn't take a lot of work, it just takes a humble heart that is ready to submit to Him and accept the gift He's offered to each one of us, the gift of salvation He provided through His death, which makes it possible for us to enter our heavenly home. I think we all need to be reminded of that familiar phrase, "Only one life, twill soon be past, only what's done for Christ will last."

# Chapter 44

$\mathscr{M}$

# Twins' Return Trip to the Philippines

Tami and Terri, along with their spouses had the privilege of going back to the Philippines in October, 2016. We as parents had the joy of following them through phone texts and pictures as well as through Facebook messages. Forty years had passed since they left the Philippines and I asked them to answer a few questions that I thought might be interesting to all. I will share their responses with you:

**What was most memorable?**

**Tami:**

I would say it was going back to the house in San Lorenzo Village, Makati where we lived when I was 9-13 years old. The street signs were made out of concrete and my brother, sister, and I would sit on that structure as we waited for the school bus every morning. The house had been updated but some of the trees were still the same along with the street, which still included the big speed bumps we always rode over with our bikes. Playing basketball in our driveway, building tree houses with our friends and having Ping-Pong tournaments on our screened-in porch were memories that came rushing back to my mind.

Our former house in Makati

We walked around the corner to find the house of our friends who also happened to be twins. We used to play Monopoly by the hour with them and bought two Dachshund puppies from their mom.

We had amazing sleepover parties in that house and many weekends where our friends that lived in the school dorm enjoyed coming to our house. The house also reminded me of how many church meetings we hosted at our home. The other memory that came back was all the great family dinners we would enjoy every night with a great meal with either mangos or saba (the cooking banana) for dessert. Following that, as a nightly routine, we had the reading of a chapter from a Danny Orlis book before prayer time. What I remember most was that we felt at home wherever we were together as a family.

**Terri:**

First of all, that we were able to go back and experience the Philippines together with our husbands and JJ was fantastic. It was always a dream to be able to have Ed and Steve see how we grew up and experience the culture and land of the Philippines.

Twins at their former school bus stop

The last day we were able to connect with some of our Filipino friends that we grew up with. The Chancos were a family in our Makati church. We were able to meet Rowena, Roxanne, and Redda at a mall in Makati. It had been over 40 years since we had seen them but it was like we picked up right where we had left off way back then. They are all serving the Lord as leaders in churches and schools and all of them were great moms to their children. They still had sweet spirits and were full of humor. The older girls used to babysit us and the younger sisters were the recipients of our hand-me-downs. We had such a great time talking at Starbucks and catching up after all those years! It was funny to watch others see how close we were with one another.

With the Chanco girls

That same evening we went back to our hotel and Gay Potente Villa met us for dinner. She grew up with us in Lucena and would come over every day to learn English while we had our homeschool lessons. She is still very prolific in English and is very successful running her own business and is an excellent wife and mother. She continues to teach Sunday School to children each week at her church. Her mother is still going strong and is well into her 80's and serves as a prayer leader at their church. She was Mom's best Filipino friend in the province.

With Gay Potente Villa

## What had changed most after forty years?

### Tami

What I found to be most different was the abundance of American and European stores where you could buy everything you would buy from home. When we lived in the Philippines, the only way we could buy goods from the States was if we could go to Clark Air Base to the commissary, which happened on very rare occasions. The other difference was the incredible number of huge malls very close together and always filled with people. When we lived there, we hardly ever ate at a restaurant and the only one I remembered was Max's (famous for their chicken). Now there is almost every chain restaurant that we have in the U.S. as well as many from Japan and other countries. Starbucks is all over the place. There were big malls in even a number of cities outside of Manila.

Going from bringing all of our possessions in barrels or crates on a ship, including our car, to now being able to purchase everything you would need or want was a big change.

The other huge change was the unbelievable traffic in Manila. We thought it was bad before but nobody could've prepared me for the unbelievably crowded streets and the crowds of people walking, streaming into the malls and piled on top of one another in shacks and make-shift houses wherever the government hadn't succeeded in relocating them to build super tall high-rises in their place. By the amount of construction and cranes stretched high in the air, you would think the economy is improving. The other big change is the enormous number of Filipino overseas workers that has hurt a lot of family structures.

**Terri**

I think the biggest change I saw was how resilient the Filipino people have been in the past forty years. The city of Manila is so large (over 21 million) and they have built on every square inch of it. There was hardly a single landmark that had stayed the same other than Manila Bay and Luneta Park. They have been building so many new skyscrapers and huge Fifth Ave elite malls. Even the provinces and outlying cities and towns have come so far with huge shopping malls to replace the open-air markets and new streets and housing developments. So many people have risen to at least a lower middle class status and are fluent with their English.

**What was the greatest blessing?**

**Tami:**

The greatest blessing was getting invited to the Conservative Baptist Global meetings. This is an organization started predominately by Filipino leaders from the Conservative Baptist Association of the Philippines or CBAP. These leaders traced their salvation and discipleship back to the missionaries I knew along with a number of them being brought to the Lord under my parents' ministry. I feel like I got to come back after forty years of planting and saw the harvest and multiplication of disciples. It was so rewarding to see the national leaders now soaring on their own with very little American missionary influence. The quality of leaders they had become and that they in turn are developing was remarkable. They each brought a next generation ministry leader with them. It was incredible to see them instigate these relationships and ministry partnerships with many other countries especially in Asia. All these global leaders have a passion for the Gospel to go forth all over the world. The intentional strategies that were developed during these meetings were ingenious and unifying. It was an amazing experience to worship and share the same God, heart, and mission with so many different cultures in one room. The friendships formed were an amazing blessing.

**Terri:**

I truly enjoyed everything we got to see and experience but the very best part of the trip was reconnecting with our friends after all these years.

**What remained pretty much the same?**

**Tami:**

Unfortunately what has stayed most the same were the huge masses of people seemingly stuck in poverty. Even though it looks like there's been a lot of economic growth, and I think there has been, there are still so many people who don't own a car so public transportation is the only option. A few light rails have been built, however, there aren't enough to serve the demand. Buses, jeepneys and tricycles are still the major source of getting around. There seems to be a larger middle class than before but there's still such a gap between the super rich and the extremely poor.

**Terri:**

To me, the thing that seemed most the same was the amazing people. They are still so hospitable and thoughtful. They are so cheerful as well as clever and innovative. No matter how difficult life is at times they faithfully rise to the occasion. Those that know the Lord as Savior are eager to share God's Word and find ways to witness for Him. In spite of their many hardships, they carry on most of the time with a smile. When we lived in Lucena, some of the provincial children taught us many fun games using our rubber thongs, rubber bands and other every day objects. The older children often cared for the younger ones and like their parents, they were very innovative, and always found a way to have fun.

Our former home in Lucena

## How did it affect your spouse?

## Tami:

My spouse had visited the Philippines thirty years ago so he was also struck with many of the same changes as I was. I think what he was most moved by was the people's hearts for reaching others and the intentional efforts they were making as an association and also partnering with the countries all over the world to spread the Gospel.

He loved watching my sister and I get excited about finding each landmark that was dear to us. I so appreciated all the efforts he made to help us find and get to each location. The trip to Lucena turned out to be an eleven-hour day. We all realized you get nowhere fast in the Philippines.

**Terri:**

I think one of the most memorable sights for Ed was the day we visited the extremely poor people who lived under the Pasig Bridge. I don't think he had ever seen such a low level of existence and was marveling at how happy the children were as they played with their homemade and imaginary toys.

People living below the Pasig Bridge

Ed, Terri, Tami, JJ, and Steve on the rock at
Faith Academy where the kids used to play

# Chapter 45

## In Retrospect

It is in looking back that I clearly see God's *Unseen Hand* at work. It is He who gave me a godly, praying mother who taught me to have confidence in God, and a father who often made me fearful and insecure. In my early years I predominately saw the negative characteristics of my father, however, God was good in giving me certain blessings so that I would have a sincere love for him in spite of his sinful life and the things he did which hurt me personally. God used my parents to mold me into the person He wanted me to be—an insecure child that desperately needed Jesus. I am thankful God allowed me to see the commendable parts of my parents' personalities as I matured in the Lord. I am supremely grateful for the transforming work He did in the life of my father in answer to our prayers. I realize now that God never intended for me to be self-sufficient. I know His riches are a perfect match for my needs and the longings and yearnings within my heart. He designed me to be incomplete without Him. I just wish it had not taken me so long to realize that amazing fact.

Recently I've been reminded of a story from my childhood that I would rather forget. I have never shared this story with anyone because I am still so ashamed that I would do something like this. However, I share it to show my appreciation for the gift of the Holy Spirit. When I was about eight or nine years old, I recall going to the Ben Franklin store downtown with about fifteen cents to spend. As a child, I was attracted to beautiful things. I have always been a bit idealistic. In this case it was nail polish in spite of the fact that it was considered, by most Christians in that day, to be worldly. I wanted it so badly and I also wanted a little makeup bag. I notice little girls of that age love small containers in which to organize their personal stuff. Both cost the amount of the money I had. I mulled this over and over in my mind and my manipulative mind told me I could put the nail polish in the makeup bag and hand it to the clerk and she would not know that I had both things but paid only for one. I took it home with me, telling no one, not even my sister. I was so convicted of my sin, I purposed in my heart to go back to the store with one of the items and return it. The clerk that dealt with me was not there that day so I took the easy route and just put the item back where I got it. I escaped having to confess to the clerk but I finally had peace in my heart. I thank God for His conviction. To this day, no one knew about that sin but God and me, but I praise God for making me miserable and for the lesson He taught me. That memory gives me proof of God's Spirit living in my heart following my salvation. I could not live with God's conviction of a sin not dealt with. It also revealed to me the evil that my flesh was capable of.

As I've grown in the faith, I realize what a great blessing it is to have God's conviction. It is a miserable state in which to be but when properly dealt with, brings hope and peace rather than haunting fear. Have I always been this sensitive to the Spirit and reacted in obedience? Sadly, there have been times I've shrugged at God and thought or did my own thing for a time, but God would never give peace until I got right with Him.

I thank God for working His ways into our family. Each of my siblings was blessed with Christian mates and their children have gone on to serve the Lord. Hildi's daughter, Darla and her husband, Mark Hetchler along with their six children, Allison, Ryan, Emily, Anna, Caleb and Jacob are active in church and all being raised to know Jesus.

Ken's daughter, Lynette and her husband Brian Nibbe, have been missionaries in Romania for over twenty years. Their three oldest sons are serving the Lord in Romania and the youngest son, Bradley, is a member of the U.S. Air Force. Ken's daughter, Lori and husband Dave Drury, serve the Lord through singing and other leadership skills. They have four children, Lauren, Hunter, Alyssa, and Colton. I will never forget Hunter's battle with leukemia as a baby, but God brought him through. He became a high school football player and an expert swimmer. Lauren is married to Trevor Koch and has two children, a son Jude and a daughter named Luna. Alyssa and Colton are also following the Lord. Ken's son, Kevin married to Suzanne is a worship leader and associate pastor. He also conducts a vocal studio in his home. Kevin has two daughters, and one son. Daughters Ellie and Sarah are studying at Liberty University and Ethan, the youngest, is still in high school. All of Ken's children have great voices as well as their mates. Lynette has recorded several CD's.

As for Glady and Tom, I know they are enjoying the babies she miscarried who I am confident are in the heavenlies with them. To God be the praise for all He has done in my family.

My home and living conditions were unique, yet God used them to prepare me to understand people in poverty, whether at home in the U.S. or in the Philippines. Those difficult conditions also showed me how far He has brought me as well as His constant love and care. It reminds me I must take nothing for granted.

Experiencing shame was one of the most difficult hurdles for me. The poverty, lack of necessities of life such as food, clothing, indoor plumbing, Dad's time spent in jail, and his drinking brought many difficulties with regard to peer pressure. As a result, I lived much of my life as a "pleaser" desiring so much to be accepted. There was a feeling of vulnerability because of the shame that hurt so severely. Yet those experiences have allowed me to experience the wonder of God's mercy and grace. Whereas I formerly was shy and dependent on others, I have learned that I am accepted and deeply loved by God and He does not call me inferior.

Too much of my life was spent forever learning to cope with my own problems and seeking to find my way in life—to know my personal path. I have found that many of the things I was ashamed of, I now value. I am able to see trials as blessings that brought me into a greater intimacy with Jesus. I have also realized the great blessing of getting my eyes off myself and onto the needs of others. God has shown me that it is not what I see in the mirror that is important but what God sees in my heart. "Sometimes we have to fail to find out who we are" as the Oak Ridge Boys so aptly sing. We often cannot believe the evil we are capable of due to pride, fear, or lack of trust.

God's loving hand was in the life partner He provided. The fact that our parents knew each other was both good and bad. Early in our relationship, I experienced feelings of rejection from Steve's family. Gradually God brought understanding and those feelings changed. Our church background was similar, yet our home life was quite different. I grew up in a small town with difficult family circumstances, whereas he lived on a farm most of his growing-up years in a stable family environment. As a result his family's food supply was plentiful most of the time. Steve experienced hard work and learned so much that I have never learned regarding farm animals, farm procedures and tools of the trade. He has used that knowledge many times in his teaching and preaching. I needed someone with experiences I didn't have and he needed my experience in secretarial skills for the ministry and my help in putting him through seminary. Added to that, God allowed both of us to serve Him in music. Opportunities came during seminary days for me to teach which was another blessing from God's hand, as I needed that experience for teaching in the Philippines and later at Southwestern College in Phoenix. God never wastes an experience. I thank God for my husband's missionary heart. He so readily interacts with people and has been a great soul-winner that has warmed my heart through the years. He was strong in so many areas where I was weak and I praise God for the thrill of singing together all these years.

Yes, even the fire was from God's hand. He taught us not to place so much value on the visible things of this world. That was a lesson I especially needed. Because of all I lacked in my younger years, I placed a great deal of value on the lovely gifts our churches had provided for us. God knew I needed to learn to lean on Him and place my values on eternal things. I have to admit that I didn't completely learn that lesson until later years; however, God often brought the fire to my mind to refresh my memory. Truly God's hand was in keeping our wedding pictures out of the fire by allowing them to be temporarily lost. This was another sign of God's love and grace in watching out for His children.

God gave us the desires of our heart when He gave us our children—our twin girls, followed by our son, Mark. God answered our prayers to provide them with the right temperaments, for they never complained about being missionary kids. They didn't feel they were missing out on things other kids had. They enjoyed each day and put up with many less than desirable circumstances and health issues. Only God could do that. I praise God most of all that they have chosen to follow God and God has rewarded each with a godly mate.

There came a day when I needed to realize that my children were first of all God's. They were not in this world to make me happy, proud, or secure. I had to release them to God and realize He had a plan for each one of them and it wasn't my place to hold them back or control their lives. The empty nest was a difficult adjustment for me. Yet in spite of my desire to have them near, I desired God's best for them and I knew my duty was to pray diligently for them. God had His hand in each of their marriages and the lives of their children who all know Jesus and have that personal relationship with Him. That is a parent's greatest joy and the opposite is a parent's greatest sorrow.

The deaths in our family were not easy to deal with but even here we saw God's hand, particularly using Glady and Tom's deaths to bring my father to salvation. I can only imagine the joy on my mother's face as she saw her prayers answered when Dad entered heaven. God knew the perfect timing in taking our loved ones home and always brought comfort and peace in each of the situations. Trials and grief, whether temporary or enduring, do not destroy the real purpose of life.

We moved several times in the Philippines and the years following. God has always provided us with a home that was suitable for our needs and allowed us to minister to both rich and poor. We learned to love them all and found something beneficial wherever He placed us.

Becoming a missionary was very different than I anticipated. I never realized how much I'd learn from those in a different culture, yes even in the field of music. I experienced the joy of ministry in music as a great means of praising God—not just an art to be achieved. I see it as a message not just to a congregation or audience, but a means of bringing joy to the heart of God. It is communicating with Him and to Him about the joy in our hearts. Someone has said, "Music is what feelings sound like." What a wonderful way to share our love to the One who gives us a song. It has been found that music imprints itself in the brain deeper than any other human experience and brings back the feeling of life when nothing else can. What a great privilege it was to work with all the wonderful missionaries in our mission. They are some of the sharpest people I've ever met.

I learned the value of suffering in that it taught me more about God's love and faithfulness. Suffering is a condition similar to a drought where the roots of the trees grow deeper as they search for water and as a result, grow stronger. God teaches us so much through trials and shows His mercy and grace in ways we would never know unless we are forced to get into His Word, claim His promises and partake of the love and comfort that He brings. It is then that He teaches us the greatest lessons and we learn that God's love is not measured by how great or how little we suffer.

Perhaps because we have been missionaries, we have been asked to deal with issues concerning demonic oppression and possession. We had never had to directly deal with this in the Philippines, however others did. To our surprise, we have found it to be very prevalent in America. We have never sought this type of ministry, but have had to deal with several very dramatic instances of this. One particular time stands out in my memory as we dealt with a young man who had to be led to our home and held down by his family. He didn't want to come and was very antagonistic. Steve sat across the room from him speaking to him in a soft voice, never laying a hand on him, and we saw a dramatic release of several demons. When the last one left, the young man stood and praised Jesus for His mighty power. He said to his father, "Dad, I'm me again." He was set free from the bondage that had enslaved him. Seeing the power in the name of Jesus is truly an awesome privilege. God allowed us to see with our own eyes the change in that young man and it is something we will never forget. It strengthened our faith greatly.

Perhaps the most valuable lesson I have learned, has come through being alone with the Lord, rather than out busily doing ministry. I have found that more has been accomplished in my life through my times with Him than any other way. Praying aloud in my devotional times and recording my praises and requests in a journal, brought new life to my interaction with Him. Over the years I have assigned certain groups of requests to each day of the week so I would not leave out certain people or situations. Above all I have learned to listen to Him as I read His Word and contemplate what He wants me to know or do. In our fast-paced, instantaneous type world, it is difficult to be still and know that He is God. Sometimes God has to *force* us to be still, in order to really hear His voice and feel His touch. But nothing brings more joy and peace.

Just before this story was finished, God gave a special blessing to my daughters along with their husbands and our grandson, JJ. It thrills our hearts that our children still love the land and people where they grew up. Tami and Steve were able to go to the Philippines for a Conservative

Baptist Global conference with Asian leaders. It was a challenging time as leaders there determined to pray for 2,016 churches to be born in 2016. They were able to participate in the sessions. The following week Terri and Ed Godoy and JJ Engram joined them as they took some time to retrace our missionary work, visit our former homes and Faith Academy where the kids attended school. Though much had changed they felt at home when they visited their old bus stop where the Faith Academy bus picked them up each day. JJ got a good look at the Philippines as he stayed on another month and did some missionary work with one of our missionary friends who by the way, attended kindergarten with the twins.

Time is a trainer in trust. God tells us to "Rest in the Lord, and wait patiently for Him" (Psalm 37:7a). He is in control, not us. It's not in trying but in trusting. He tells us to "rest" in Him. It sounds so effortless—almost lackadaisical, yet it is one of the most difficult tasks in life. Why? I believe it's because of our flesh that wants to exalt itself thinking, "surely there is something I can do!" But Jesus tells us to come as little children. As simple as it sounds, it has taken me years to fully understand this concept, and sadly, I haven't fully learned it yet. Sensing God's hand and answers to prayer does not come because of an exemplary life on our part. It is only because of His promises to provide His mercy and grace to those who believe in Him and diligently seek Him. It is human nature to want to know what God is doing behind the scenes as we wait on Him. It is then we must be reminded, "When you can't see His plan, and you can't trace His hand, trust His heart."

God's Word showed me in many ways that He wanted me to share my story just as Asaph of old who said, "I will speak to you in a parable. I will teach you hidden lessons from our past—stories we have heard and known, stories our ancestors handed down to us. We will not hide these truths from our children; we will tell the next generation about the glorious deeds of the LORD, about His power and His mighty wonders. For he issued his laws to Jacob; he gave his instructions to Israel. He commanded our ancestors to teach them to their children, so the next generation might know them—even the children not yet born—and they in turn will teach their own children. So each generation should set its hope anew on God, not forgetting His glorious miracles and obeying His commands. Then they will not be like their ancestors—stubborn, rebellious, and unfaithful, refusing to give their hearts to God" (Psalms 78:2b-7 NLT). Do you have a story to share? God wants us to see His matchless love and character through every day and often these come through trials uniquely disguised as blessings led by His unseen hand.

Printed in the United States
By Bookmasters